SECRET MICHIGAN

A Guide to the Weird, Wonderful, and Obscure

Amy Piper

REEDY PRESS

Reedy Press
PO Box 5131
St. Louis, MO 63139
www.reedypress.com

Library of Congress Control Number: 2023951946
ISBN: 9781681065281

Design by Jill Halpin

Unless otherwise indicated, all photos are courtesy of the author or in the public domain.

We (the publisher and the author) have done our best to provide the most accurate information available when this book was completed. However, we make no warranty, guarantee, or promise about the accuracy, completeness, or currency of the information provided, and we expressly disclaim all warranties, express or implied. Please note that attractions, company names, addresses, websites, and phone numbers are subject to change or closure, and this is outside of our control. We are not responsible for any loss, damage, injury, or inconvenience that may occur due to the use of this book. When exploring new destinations, please do your homework before you go. You are responsible for your own safety and health when using this book.

Printed in the United States of America
25 26 27 28   5 4 3 2

To my favorite exploration partners: my husband, Ross; my daughter, Alexis; and my two granddaughters, Cassidy and Lyric.

They're always up for an adventure!

Pictured Rocks National Lakeshore

CONTENTS

Brys Estate
Photo courtesy of the
Secret Garden at Brys Estate

ACKNOWLEDGMENTS

Thank you to my family for their support during the entire process of authoring this book. I know they loved exploring some of these secrets as much as I did; however, in the end, they took turns as the journey was long. I'm sure they would have instead been pursuing their interests rather than tagging along on some of the long drives we took around the state.

I'm not sure I would have authored this book without the inspiration of Roxie Yonkey of RoxieontheRoad.com and the author of *Secret Kansas*. The year before I wrote *Secret Michigan*, I found myself tagging along on a road trip with Roxie, and it was during that trip I discovered how much fun uncovering a state's secrets can be. Thank you, Roxie!

Thank you to everyone who shared their secrets with me—some were so deep and dark that I wouldn't have discovered them without a tip-off.

A special thanks to all the destinations that shared the secrets of their locations.

Grand Traverse Commons

INTRODUCTION

What's surprising is how many secrets Michigan hides behind the well-known destinations. The mysteries it keeps, places you may have been, but things you never noticed. Stories that only the locals know. Places the locals didn't want me to reveal. Occasionally, they would request that I not disclose an exact location for fear of spoiling it.

The weird—a lighthouse on the move, haunted lighthouses and breweries, and a restaurant dedicated to chicken gizzards are only a few of the strange things you'll find in Michigan. The wonderful—waterfalls, national shorelines, and lakeshores are expected in a state that is second in the nation only to Alaska in miles of shoreline, yet they have their own secrets. And then, the obscure—shipwrecks below the Great Lakes, endangered species, secret gardens, and hidden lakes all made the list. While everyone may know about the Detroit Institute of Arts and Frederik Meijer Gardens & Sculpture Park, do you know about the local historical museums that are there to tell the story of Michigan's past? Kings and castles are all part of the state's history.

For this book, a secret may be a surprising backstory behind a well-known attraction, the world's largest, most miniature, and unusual food—things that make you exclaim, "That's weird!"

As a lifelong resident of Michigan, even I was surprised at what I didn't know. Harry Blackstone, Thomas Alva Edison, and Sojourner Truth—historical figures I associated with other places whom I discovered had roots in Michigan.

While Michigan's Upper Peninsula and Detroit have dedicated *Secret* books, I couldn't leave out those areas entirely from a book on secret Michigan. For even more secrets, check out those books that do a deep dive into those areas of my beloved state.

GOD SAVE THE KING

Who is the only king to have ruled in the United States?

While James Jesse Strang, born in 1813, wasn't of royal blood, at about age 19, he contacted Queen Victoria of England, expressing a love interest. When he didn't receive a reply, he took a different approach to reaching the throne. Instead, he would create his own kingdom and proclaim himself king.

It began when Joseph Smith founded Mormonism in western New York. As the Mormons moved west to avoid religious persecution, Smith met Strang. As Strang became part of Smith's inner circle, Smith assigned him to establish a community of followers in Voree, Wisconsin.

In 1844, when an angry mob murdered Joseph Smith, leaving the Mormon Church's leadership position open, Brigham Young was the heir apparent. However, James Strang provided a letter ostensibly written by Joseph Smith naming him his successor. While most Mormons chose to follow Brigham Young to Salt Lake, some followers remained with Strang.

It was 1847 when a commoner, a farmer named James Jesse Strang, stepped off the boat onto Beaver Island. As the number of followers grew, so did his arrogance, and on July 8, 1850, he proclaimed himself king.

Under Strang's direction, the Print Shop published two newspapers, the *Northern Islander*, and the *Daily Northern*

BEAVER ISLAND PRINT SHOP MUSEUM

WHAT: A printshop built by Strang's followers, now a historical museum telling the story of Beaver Island's history, including James Jesse Strang's era

WHERE: 26275 Main St., Beaver Island

COST: Free, donations accepted

PRO TIP: Visit the shoreline area across from the museum where two disgruntled followers assassinated King Strang.

Top: *Beaver Island Print Shop Museum on Beaver Island.*
Inset: *A picture of James Jesse Strang inside the Beaver Island Print Shop Museum.*

Islander. Soon, he was dictating island life. The breaking point came in 1851 when the "consecration of spoils" was promoted, permitting Mormons to steal from non-Mormons on the island.

By the following year, Strang had total control of the island and decreed that non-Mormons must join the church or leave Beaver Island. All left by November. Strang continued to rule for the next four years.

On June 16, 1856, two disgruntled followers assassinated King Strang. Shortly after his death, all Mormons on Beaver Island were rounded up, escorted to ships in the harbor, and removed. That was the end of Mormon rule on Beaver Island.

In addition to the Print Shop Museum, Beaver Island offers other attractions that provide more insight into the island's history: the Beaver Island Marine Museum, Protar's Home, Heritage Park, and the lighthouses.

HAIL TO THE CHIEF

Who was the only president who was also a king?

In Omaha, Nebraska, Dorothy Ayer Gardner King and Leslie Lynch King became a family of three on July 14, 1913. They named their son Leslie Lynch King Jr. Two weeks later, escaping an abusive relationship, Dorothy and her infant son left Nebraska. In December 1913, the Omaha courts finalized her divorce from Leslie King. In 1914, she relocated to Grand Rapids, Michigan, to live with her parents.

On February 1, 1917, Dorothy King married Gerald R. Ford Sr., a Grand Rapids businessman who sold paint. Although Ford didn't formally adopt the young boy, Dorothy and Ford Sr. began calling their son Gerald R. Ford Jr.

Ford had known since he was 13 that Gerald Ford Sr. was not his biological father. However, it wasn't until 1930, when Leslie King visited Grand Rapids, that the young Ford had an unplanned meeting with this biological father.

After his paternal grandparents passed, Ford took the legal steps to officially become Gerald R. Ford Jr. on December 3, 1935.

In 1972, the people elected Ford to his 13th and final term as a congressman from Michigan.

Gerald R. Ford Jr. became the 38th president of the United States of America. He was never on the ballot for vice president, but Congress appointed him following Spiro Agnew's resignation and confirmed him on December 6, 1973. Finally, he became the only president of the United States never elected when Richard Nixon resigned on August 9, 1974.

Ford graduated from the University of Michigan, Ann Arbor, in 1935 with a BA in economics. Ford played center on the university's football team.

Top: *The Gerald R. Ford Presidential Museum in Grand Rapids.* Inset: *The Gerald R. Ford Presidential Library in Ann Arbor. Inset photo courtesy of Alexis Dingman*

On January 20, 1977, Ford left office following a loss in the general election to Jimmy Carter.

GERALD R. FORD PRESIDENTIAL MUSEUM

WHAT: A presidential museum with a collection of historical artifacts telling the story of Gerald R. Ford's life

WHERE: 303 Pearl St. NW, Grand Rapids

COST: Adults, $12; senior citizens and military service members, $10; college students with ID, $9; youth ages 6–18, $6; children 5 and under, free

PRO TIP: While the Gerald R. Ford Presidential Museum is in Grand Rapids, the Gerald R. Ford Presidential Library is in Ann Arbor.

THE SISTERHOOD OF DOLLS

How did a little girl's childhood pastime mature into receiving a papal blessing?

In a northern Michigan wood, where the world's largest crucifix rises from among the trees, another example of "the largest" stature sits on the lower level of the shrine's church: the largest collection of more than 525 nun dolls and 20 mannequins started in 1945 as a childhood hobby.

As a girl of about 8, Sally Rogalski (née Traub) began dressing her dolls as nuns in their traditional habits. As time passed, it became her way of preserving some of the Catholic Church's history. During the 1960s, after Vatican II, most religious communities switched from traditional habits to plain clothes and added a pin or cross representing their specific congregation or order. However, Sally continued to dress her dolls in their traditional habits, representing various orders and ministries.

After their marriage, Sally's husband, Wally Rogalski, supported her passion and even built display cases to showcase the dolls. In 1964, the Rogalskis donated 230 dolls to the shrine, stipulating that the church could never charge an admission fee, ensuring everyone could enjoy the dolls regardless of financial standing. After the initial donation, Sally continued to dress dolls

THE NUN DOLL MUSEUM AT CROSS IN THE WOODS SHRINE

WHAT: The nation's most extensive collection of nun dolls dressed in traditional habits

WHERE: 7078 M-68, Indian River

COST: Free

PRO TIP: The shrine doesn't allow pets on its grounds.

as nuns with the help of the orders they represented. Her contributions continued until 525 dolls became part of the collection. The collection is the largest in the United States, representing Diocesan clergy and over 217 sisters, priests, and brothers religious orders worldwide. You'll find dolls representing Mother Teresa, the Sisters of Mercy, and the Franciscans, to name a few.

The Nun Doll Exhibit in Indian River, Michigan

Their efforts didn't go unnoticed, and in 1988, Sally and Wally received a papal blessing from Pope John Paul II for promoting vocations in the priesthood and religious life. Today, the nun doll collection is a testament to Sally's childhood hobby and dedication to preserving the Catholic Church's history.

The Man on the Cross is a Marshall Fredericks–designed sculpture constructed from Oregon redwood that grew when Jesus walked the earth. The cross is 55 feet tall and 22 feet wide. The bronze body weighs seven tons and is 28 feet tall.

THE SECRET GARDEN

How did a husband-wife entrepreneurial team who worked and lived in the same place maintain a work–life balance?

Eileen and Walter Brys retired from corporate jobs and decided to pursue their dream of owning a winery. So, the Brys Estate Vineyard & Winery became the entrepreneurs' family business and home. That dual function made it difficult to escape the day-to-day, to have some downtime, to reflect and connect. So, they ran from the demands to a spot hidden on the estate.

Following the curve in the path, down a hill, and around a bend sits a 12-acre parcel of land too low to grow grapes. Even cherry trees didn't do well in this area of the estate. A tucked-away place that people didn't realize was there. That became Eileen and Walter's escape—their secret spot. After a while, they saw the potential of sharing their private getaway.

Lavender and grapes grow well together in Provence, so they started with 1,000 lavender plants and opened to the public in 2016. Today, the Secret Garden grows nine varieties of English lavender, U-pick strawberries, a U-cut flower garden, and an herb garden. In addition, they grow sage, peppermint, and lemon balm in the herb garden.

They purchased a former church property. Today, they make lavender products for their gift shop in the former church hall.

The Secret Garden allows families to reconnect and cancer patients to reflect and enjoy nature. You'll find rocking chairs,

---

The Wine Wagon Tour & Tasting is a two-hour experience that takes you to five locations throughout the 155-acre estate winery via an electric shuttle. This excursion includes a stop at the Secret Garden.

The Secret Garden at Brys Estate in Traverse City. Photo courtesy of the Secret Garden at Brys Estate

benches, a patio area, and picnic tables. Bring a picnic lunch and sample their signature lavender ice cream made at the Traverse City local manufacturer, Moomers, as dessert. The lavender shortbread cookies are another snack option for your road trip home or as a dessert for your picnic.

The Brys Estate Vineyard & Winery started as an unattainable dream that worked out.

BRYS ESTATE VINEYARD & WINERY

WHAT: A secluded garden growing lavender, perennial flowers, strawberries, and herbs tucked away from the tasting room and winery

WHERE: 3309 Blue Water Rd., Traverse City

COST: Free to visit; purchase prices vary.

PRO TIP: The Secret Garden is open Memorial Day through October 30. The lavender field is most spectacular during the first three weeks of July.

THE SHORELINE'S TINY TREASURE IS IN PERIL

What happened to the piping plover, and how are organizations aiding its comeback?

Charadrius melodus is an endangered shorebird commonly known as the piping plover. The Great Plains, the Atlantic Coast, and the Great Lakes have small piping plover populations. While they summer separately during the breeding season, they winter together on the Gulf Coast. In 1986, piping plovers flew onto the federal endangered species list. At one point, the Great Lakes had almost 800 pairs of piping plovers, but by 1990, that number had dropped to 13. Today, Sleeping Bear Dunes National Lakeshore is home to the most significant number of piping plovers in the Great Lakes, where you'll find between 75 and 80 nesting pairs throughout the Great Lakes region.

These tiny treasures wear white pants and a sand-colored topcoat, so their beachy environment perfectly camouflages them. In addition, piping plovers only nest on beaches, with a preference for those with gravel.

Habitat loss and predators are the two primary reasons the Great Lakes population has become endangered. In addition, their beach nesting areas have become recreational and developed areas for humans. Domestic animals and wild predators kill piping plovers and destroy their eggs.

SLEEPING BEAR DUNES NATIONAL LAKESHORE

WHAT: The Great Lakes population of the piping plover

WHERE: Visitor center, 9922 Front St., Empire

COST: National Park Service standard entrance pass, $15–$25

PRO TIP: Schedule a guided walking tour of the piping plovers and their habitat with Sleeping Bear Tour Co. from May through July.

Top: *A Piping Plover at Sleeping Bear Dunes National Lakeshore.* Inset: *Piping Plover nests with protective covering.*

Wildlife monitors begin watching their activities when the piping plovers return in spring. Once these birds establish their nesting territories, workers rope off nesting areas to protect them. Once a worker discovers a nest, trained staff build a wire fence with a mesh top, preventing predators from damaging the eggs and allowing plovers to access their nests easily. This practice prevents the eggs from accidentally being crushed by beach walkers who don't notice them. It also stops any interference that may result in the birds abandoning their nests.

Many organizations are working together to aid the recovery of these tiny treasures. The Great Lakes Piping Plover Conservation Team works toward this common goal. State and federal agencies, nongovernmental organizations, the Great Lakes tribes, universities, and private citizens make up the team.

While you're bird-watching, obey the fenced-off areas. Then, enjoy the plovers from a distance. Leave your pets at home. If you find a plover family outside the fencing, give it space. The tiny chicks are easily stepped on accidentally.

A PLACE OF HEALING

How did a state hospital become one of the nation's largest historic preservation projects?

It was the early 1880s when mule power and hand tools were the only means of construction available. More than 60 years would pass before the first psychiatric drugs would exist.

In April 1883, construction began on the Victorian Italianate–style main building, Building 50. They used over eight million bricks from the local brickyard at Cedar Lake, about three miles north of the site. In November 1885, the Northern Michigan Asylum, later renamed the Traverse City State Hospital, admitted its first patient. Dr. James Decker Munson, founding medical superintendent, followed the revolutionary moral treatment movement. "Beauty is therapy" was a central component of the treatment plan: surround patients with a beautiful environment, and their mental and emotional states would improve.

Architects designed the facility according to the Kirkbride Plan—each patient room had a window and an outside view. Ample natural light was essential. Hospital staff served patient meals in the dining room on fine china, complete with the state seal. White linen tablecloths and fresh flowers adorned the tables. The staff decorated the asylum's walls with inspirational sayings and art.

Finally, during the mid-1900s, a few comparatively minor fire code defects in the administration section of Building 50, referred to as Old Center, led to its demolition approval in 1963. They constructed a new two-story, flat-roof building in its place, now called the Village Center. Then, over the next 30 years, the

---

Situated on 480 acres of preserved parklands, you'll find 140 acres of unpaved trails for year-round hiking, biking, and cross-country skiing.

An aerial view of Grand Traverse Commons today. Photo courtesy of Grand Traverse Commons

community and state debated demolishing or preserving the rest of Building 50.

After 104 years, the Traverse City State Hospital closed its doors in 1989 and remained vacant until 2000. The elements and vandals took their toll on the once-beautiful campus. In 2002, the Minervini Group acquired the property and began one of the nation's largest historic preservation and adaptive reuse developments.

Today, a bakery's brick oven fire burns in one of the former firehouses. In another, you'll find a restaurant featuring Mexican food. The hospital's laundry has become a dual-use winery and coffee roastery. The former chapel is now Kirkbride Hall, a community gathering space. The main building has become apartments, shops, and restaurants, creating a new community in this former place of healing.

THE VILLAGE AT GRAND TRAVERSE COMMONS

WHAT: One of the nation's most extensive historic preservation and adaptive reuse redevelopment projects

WHERE: 1200 W 11th St., Traverse City

COST: Free to visit. Tours and purchase prices vary.

PRO TIP: Grand Traverse Commons offers several tours that take you through the 1885 brick steam tunnels and the rest of the grounds, providing insight into the history of this historic facility.

FROM SPIRITUALITY TO BASEBALL

Why couldn't the House of David baseball team play against major-league teams?

Benjamin and Mary Purnell founded the House of David religious colony in 1903. Benjamin taught Christianity in a slightly different way that drew people from every corner of the globe. Those who joined the House of David gave up all of their worldly possessions for the promise of everlasting life on widow.

The critical elements of their Christian-based religion were a communal, vegetarian, and celibate lifestyle. They believed that living this life would bring you everlasting life on earth. Your body would never die, living in a 1,000-year paradise. Members arrived from as far away as Australia.

This promise had tens of thousands of converts, and the House of David amassed wealth and talent. Their assets included a diamond mine in Sydney, Australia; a gold mine in western Oklahoma; a coal mine in Kentucky; and 100,000 acres of farmland throughout Michigan and Indiana.

In 1908, the religious colony completed a pre-Disneyland-style amusement park called Eden Springs Park. By 1913, they were the leading amusement park in America, second only to

HOUSE OF DAVID BASEBALL & HISTORICAL MUSEUM

WHAT: A museum owned by a local historian, Chris Siriano, that tells the stories surrounding the House of David

WHERE: 922 Main St., Saint Joseph

COST: Adult admission is $10.

PRO TIP: The museum is open by appointment only. Call Chris Siriano at 269-325-0039 or email houseofdavid9@aol.com to book an appointment.

Top: *Baseball paraphernalia from the House of David baseball team.* Inset: *One of the small-scale steam engine trains from Eden Springs Amusement Park.*

Coney Island. It was a giant attraction that operated for 71 years. The park included 11 small-scale steam-engine trains, a zoo, pony rides, hotels, and restaurants. Through the years, 35 million people visited.

In 1914, Purnell decided to form a baseball team. They had a talented and famous team comprised of White men with long hair and beards. Due to their religious beliefs, they couldn't shave or cut their hair, so they weren't allowed to play against the major-league teams. As a result, they played in the Negro Leagues. Babe Ruth even came to play with the House of David team for several games.

Music also played a central role within the community. Of the 84 Australians who joined the community, some were the best musicians in the world. Ultimately, they taught others and formed many types of performing music groups.

FROM AGRICULTURE TO ARCHITECTURE

How did a dairy farm become the idyllic setting for the fairy-tale-like castle?

Castle Farms began in 1918 as a working dairy farm called Loeb Farms. Albert Loeb, the acting president of Sears, Roebuck, and Co., built the farm to test the farm equipment sold in the Sears and Roebuck catalog. It wasn't the style of the typical northern Michigan dairy farm.

Loeb loved castles and patterned his farm's buildings after the stone castles and barns in Normandy, France. At one time, the dairy farm was Charlevoix County's largest employer, employing more than 90 workers. Their herd included more than 200 award-winning Holstein Friesian cattle. They also had 26 Belgian draft horses. The farm even had a baseball team called the Sodbusters.

In 1962, the farm became Castle Van Haver when John Van Haver bought 100 acres of the original Loeb Farms. Four years later, Van Haver opened it to the public with a café and an art gallery and conducted property tours.

In 1969, the Reibels bought the property, and after several incarnations, it became Castle Farms Summer Music Theater. The concert venue hosted many famous artists from the 1970s through the early 1990s, including the Doobie Brothers and Aerosmith.

CASTLE FARMS

WHAT: A castle set among stunning gardens and grounds that also has a model railroad and World War I museum

WHERE: 5052 M-66, Charlevoix

COST: Teens and adults ages 13–64, $20; seniors 65+ and military ID, $18; children, $15; children 2 and under, free

PRO TIP: Hours occasionally change due to special events scheduled, so check their website or call before planning your trip.

Finally, in 2001, Linda Mueller bought Castle Farms and started extensive restoration. She replaced the roofs, added wings back according to original blueprints, and created the now extensive gardens.

Today, Castle Farms makes a beautiful day trip that offers things to do for the entire family. First, stop by the theater off the lobby to watch a film on the history of Castle Farms. It shows detailed film footage about the castle's dramatic renovation.

They have Michigan's largest outdoor model railway, a World War I museum, a wine-tasting room, and a café featuring Michigan wines. In addition to the self-guided tours, Castle Farms offers guided tours daily, June through August. An additional charge applies for guided tours. They include tram rides for all tour guests at no additional charge.

The same day Albert Loeb finished construction on his farm—November 11, 1918—the Allies signed the World War I Armistice. Castle Farms turned the original blacksmith shop into a museum that tells the story of daily life during World War I.

Photo courtesy of Castle Farms Serenity Garden

PICTURE THIS

What are petroglyphs, and where can you find them in Michigan?

Petroglyphs are pictures carved into the rock, while petrographs are rock paintings. You can find petroglyphs throughout the world; however, the ones found in Sanilac Petroglyphs Historic State Park are the only known ones in Michigan.

Located in Michigan's Thumb region, near Cass City, sits the 240-acre site. The park showcases Michigan's largest known group of Native American wisdom carved in stone. The carvings are called Ezhibiigaadek Asin, meaning "written on stone" in the Anishinaabemowin language. These carvings were etched into a large sandstone outcrop along the Cass River. The exact age of the petroglyphs is uncertain, but they are believed to date back 1,500 years.

The petroglyphs depict various images—humans, animals, and abstract designs. Each carving has cultural and spiritual significance for the Native American tribe who created them. These carvings were a form of storytelling, communication, and artistic expression, providing a window into the lives of those who made them.

Early settlers discovered this significant example of petroglyphs in 1889 after a forest fire revealed the large Marshall sandstone rock. Today, it is protected by a shelter and covered in the offseason to avoid further erosion of the engravings.

The state park also has a mile-long, self-guided hiking trail loop. You'll see a 110-year-old white pine, the state tree, and what remains of a 19th-century logging camp.

Signage at Sanilac Petroglyphs State Park

You'll need to walk about a quarter mile on a hard-packed limestone, accessible trail to see the petroglyphs. They offer free guided tours to help you understand this historic site. Archaeologists believe that this wasn't a permanent village because they found few artifacts at this site. The park is on the National Register of Historic Places.

SANILAC PETROGLYPHS HISTORIC STATE PARK

WHAT: A historic Michigan state park showcasing petroglyphs

WHERE: 8251 Germania Rd., Cass City

COST: Free. A Michigan State Park Recreation Passport isn't required.

PRO TIP: The petroglyphs' viewing area is in a covered enclosure that is open seasonally, Wednesday through Sunday, Memorial Day through Labor Day.

A SYMPHONY OF NATURE

How did the Nature Megaphone come to northern Michigan?

Located in a forest clearing in Estonia's Võru County, you'll find three giant megaphones arranged as an Estonian art installation. The Estonian art project, called RUUP, stemmed from architectural students consulting with an acoustic expert to create the perfect construct to amplify the forest's sounds. That became the basis for the single nature megaphone at Banwell Nature Preserve.

The Nature Megaphone officially rests on Boyd B. Banwell Nature Preserve. You can easily enter it from the adjacent Agnes S. Andreae Nature Preserve. As visitors sit inside the wooden megaphone and listen carefully, the megaphone amplifies the sounds of the forest—birds, insects, and wind—to the point where barely audible sounds become easily heard.

The project started when Little Traverse Conservancy team member Charles Dawley learned of the original three nature megaphones in the Estonian forest. Then, at Banwell Nature Preserve, he led a team of local students from the Petoskey High School building trades class to build one of these unique structures in the United States. Home Depot donated the materials needed.

NATURE MEGAPHONE

WHAT: A large wooden structure shaped like a megaphone that you can crawl inside to hear nature's sounds amplified

WHERE: Dunn Rd., Afton

COST: Free

PRO TIP: From Indian River, take M-68 east about 5.3 miles. Look for parking and the sign on the left. Park at Andreae's parking lot and hike the two-mile loop to experience northern Michigan's forests.

Nature Megaphone

Boyd B. Banwell sold the original 320 acres in 2000. Since then, the conservancy has acquired additional parcels with more river frontage, allowing extended trails.

Banwell B. Nature Preserve, 400 acres adjacent to the Andreae Nature Preserve, features three miles of shoreline along the Pigeon River. To reach the megaphone, the closest place to park is at the Andreae Nature Preserve. The walk is approximately a two-mile round trip from the parking lot to the megaphone.

Overlooking the bluff inside the megaphone provides an excellent view above the treetops. In addition, the megaphone will amplify the wind, birdsongs, and insects buzzing for a fantastic symphony to accompany the landscape tinted with dazzling fall colors.

Hiking through Banwell Nature Preserve to see the Nature Megaphone is an excellent opportunity for fall color. The three-mile area along the Pigeon River has steep bluffs high above the river, which makes for stunning treetop views.

DRIVEN BY BEAUTY

Where have all the hood ornaments gone?

Nestled within the Gilmore Car Museum's extensive collection lies a treasure trove of rare and unique hood ornaments, offering visitors a captivating glimpse into the world of lesser-known automobiles. The exhibit, called *The Automotive Mascot*, proudly showcases hood ornaments that have become veritable automotive gems. These exquisite pieces of automotive art showcase the ingenuity, craftsmanship, and creative spirit of bygone eras, shedding light on the diverse landscape of the automotive industry.

As visitors journey through the museum's collection, they discover a fascinating array of hood ornaments that once adorned the radiators of vehicles long forgotten. Automobile designs have changed over the years. In the early 20th century, car hoods had radiator caps protruding from them. They were front, center, and unattractive. So, manufacturers designed hood ornaments to transform the radiator caps into something beautiful. Today, those caps hide underneath the hood, so hood ornaments are no longer needed to disguise the radiator caps. Each hood ornament tells a story, inviting enthusiasts and history buffs to explore the forgotten corners of automotive history.

Intricately designed and meticulously crafted, they capture the essence of each brand, reflecting their aspirations and unique design philosophies. From the sleek and streamlined

Duesenberg at the Gilmore Car Museum

forms of forgotten luxury cars to the whimsical and playful figures adorning early concept vehicles, each ornament tells a tale of innovation and ambition.

Visitors may stumble upon the captivating emblem of a defunct automaker that challenged convention or the exquisite mascot representing a groundbreaking technological advancement.

These artifacts offer a captivating journey through time, unearthing the stories of forgotten brands and celebrating the creativity and innovation that shaped the industry. Whether it's the emblem of a long-lost luxury car or the whimsical figure on an experimental vehicle, each hood ornament serves as a window into the past, allowing us to appreciate automobiles' diverse and fascinating histories.

Several factors contributed to the disappearance of hood ornaments, including safety regulations, streamlined designs, changing design trends, and cost and manufacturing efficiency.

While hood ornaments have largely disappeared from mainstream automobile design, their legacy remains preserved in the Gilmore Car Museum's collections as reminders of a bygone era when automotive artistry and individuality took center stage on the automotive hoods.

GILMORE CAR MUSEUM

WHAT: A car museum that tells the history of America through cars

WHERE: 6865 W Hickory Rd., Hickory Corners

COST: Adults and seniors, $20; youth ages 11–17, $12; active military with ID, free; children 10 and under, free

PRO TIP: From April 1 through October 31, rustic camping is available on the museum grounds.

Another fun exhibit at the museum is *Born to Perform: The Era of the Muscle Car*. The exhibition showcases cars, like Chevelles and Super Bees, with big engines and even bigger performance.

FROM BARS TO BRUSHES

How did the world's largest walled prison become a residential community for artists?

In the early 1800s, Michigan towns were vying for the critical elements of the state's infrastructure, the capital, the universities, and the prison. Ultimately, Lansing won the bid for the capital city and Ann Arbor, the University of Michigan. Many small towns desperately wanted the prison due to its associated inexpensive labor.

Michigan's first state prison, built in 1842, held 2,000 prisoners, making it the largest walled prison in the world. Jackson became one of the leading industrial cities between Detroit and Chicago, partly due to the cheap labor. The prisoners made wagon wheels, twine, and other farm implements. Some prisoners were tailors who made wedding dresses.

While the community attended concerts and other events on the prison lawn, they had no idea the atrocities that occurred hidden from the public. Prisoners weren't allowed to speak. Living conditions didn't include plumbing, heating, or cool air-conditioning. The conditions were torturous, with four punishments: privilege removal, the whipping post, one week in the iron cap, and the ball and chain.

ARMORY ARTS VILLAGE

WHAT: Jackson Historic Prison Tour

WHERE: 100 Armory Ct., Jackson

COST: A guided tour is $89 for up to three people. Free to explore the exterior grounds.

PRO TIP: Armory Arts Village is a residential area. The best way for visitors to explore the grounds is on a guided tour.

Top: *The original exterior of the world's largest prison.* Inset: *The prison today, reinvented as an artists' community.*

The need for a new prison became apparent as the inmate population grew. The State Prison of Southern Michigan opened in 1934 and could hold 5,700 inmates.

Eventually, the original prison became a National Guard armory. During that time, workers removed many of the original prison details. The National Guard vacated the building in 1996, leaving the building empty until the early '00s.

From criminal minds to creative minds, today the building features 62 combination work-and-living spaces for artists of all types. You'll still find segments of the original 25-foot wall and the castle-like turrets on the grounds. The 19-acre Armory Arts Village is the only former prison in the world repurposed as a residential community comprised of workspaces, galleries, and apartments focused on the arts.

Stop by the art gallery adjacent to the apartment building, once the wagon wheel factory, to enjoy some of the local artists' work.

WHEN CADILLAC WAS KISSED

How did a hall-of-fame rock band turn around a small-town football team's losing season?

It all started in 1975 with the Cadillac Viking football team. Coming off a winning season the previous year, the team had two losses. That's when assistant football coach Jim Neff turned to the outrageous rock band from New York City on the cusp of superstardom, KISS, for inspiration and motivation for his team. Football parlance frequently uses the term KISS—Keep It Simple, Stupid—so Coach Neff believed it was the

The 8-foot-tall monument to commemorate the 40th anniversary of KISS's homecoming attendance.

KISS knew that northern Michigan received lots of snow in winter. The band first invented and used the KISS snowstorm in Cadillac. During the final song, "Rock and Roll All Nite," their special effects team unfurled a tarp while compressed air blew confetti into the crowd, and confetti snow buried concertgoers in the first KISS snowstorm.

The Old City Hall where KISS posed for their photo op.

THE CADILLAC KISSTORY TOUR

WHAT: Music fans can walk from plaque to plaque, retracing the band's steps from 1975.

WHERE: Begins at Veterans Memorial Stadium, 400 Linden St., Cadillac

COST: Free

PRO TIP: Download the "KISStory Self-Guided Tour" PDF, which includes a map of the stops on the tour. You can also drive between the major stops if the walk is too long.

perfect match. It was so perfect that the team went on to a winning season just by having KISS's music played in the locker room before the game.

Coach Neff reached out to the rock band to let them know how their music was turning around the team's performance. They were ecstatic that their music was inspiring the team. A friendship developed between Neff and the band. A year later, a tour brought the band to Michigan. Coach Neff contacted KISS again, requesting the band appear at Cadillac's homecoming. They went to Cadillac, played a concert in the Cadillac High School gym, joined the homecoming parade, and received a key to the city from the city council.

In 2015, to celebrate the 40th anniversary of KISS's homecoming attendance, the town erected an eight-foot-tall monument to commemorate the event. The tribute includes pictures of the memorable day.

Visitors can experience the Cadillac KISStory Tour, a two-and-a-half-mile walking tour of four Cadillac KISStorical sites that have become notable since the KISS visit to Cadillac.

FLYING HIGH AT THE ZOO

Why is an aerospace and science center referred to as a zoo?

One might think that the term Air Zoo comes from the museum's location in Kalamazoo—one unusual name to go with another. However, that's not the case.

Pete and Suzanne Parish, cofounders of the Air Zoo, both had backgrounds in aviation. Sue served with the Women Airforce Service Pilots (WASP), while Pete was a former World War II Marine Air Corps aviator. It began in 1959 when Pete bought half interest in a single-engine C35 Bonanza, and then the couple bought a Stearman biplane. Their following collectibles were an AT-6 and then a Grumman Wildcat. Notice the animal reference in the Grumman.

Then Sue heard about a partially assembled P-40, a combat plane she had dreamed of flying during her WASP service. The desert-pink Flying Tiger became her trademark plane and now hangs in the Air Zoo's atrium.

When a friend gave them his Grumman Bearcat on the condition they open a museum, the couple enthusiastically agreed.

Suzanne Parish's Curtiss P-40 warhawk hanging in the lobby of the Air Zoo, also called the Flying Tiger

In November 1979, the Kalamazoo Aviation History Museum opened. People began referring to the museum as the Air Zoo because the original collection of airplanes had animal names—Flying Tiger, Bearcat, Hellcat, and Wildcat.

Today, the more-than-100,000-square-foot zoo has expanded from cats to birds. Their collection includes the only SR-71B Blackbird in the world.

The Flight Innovation Center features more than 100 aircraft, spacecraft, rides, interactive exhibits, and a theater. The Flight Discovery Center displays more than 40 aircraft from the World War II, Cold War, Korean War, and Vietnam War eras. This collection includes homebuilt planes and engines, civilian planes, and stealth aircraft.

AIR ZOO AEROSPACE & SCIENCE CENTER

WHAT: An interactive aerospace and science center with amusement-park-style rides

WHERE: Flight Innovation Center, 6151 Portage Rd., Portage; Flight Discovery Center, 3101 E Milham Rd., Kalamazoo

COST: Adults, $15.95; seniors 60+, $12.95; youth ages 5–18, $14.95; US military and veteran discount, 50% off; children 4 and under, free; parking at both sites is free.

PRO TIP: The Air Zoo offers daily electric shuttle service between the two centers. The shuttle is free to Air Zoo guests and is wheelchair accessible.

Explore the historic aircraft exhibited on the Air Zoo outdoor grounds. The Air Zoo also has a picnic area to enjoy watching airplanes take off from the local airport while eating lunch.

OH, HELL YES!

How did a small town become known as Hell?

Mr. William Kirtland founded the town of Pinckney in 1837. Shortly after, Kirtland asked his friend Mr. George Reeves from the Catskills in New York State to come to Pinkney and run his general store. Once Reeves arrived in 1838, he acquired another 1,000 acres of land, including a water element. This land would eventually become a separate town. He built a sawmill, a grist mill, and a distillery on the banks of what is now called Hell Creek.

After the Civil War, the taxman would come around to collect taxes. Liquor required additional taxes. Rumor is that Mr. Reeves paid the farmers for their grain with home-distilled whiskey. During that time, the farmers would come to town, and their horses would go home without them because they were partying in the general store, which now had a second level. The second floor included women and alcohol. The environment had become cheap and shady.

HELL, MICHIGAN

WHAT: A small, playful village with a population of under 300 that plays up the name at every opportunity

WHERE: Screams Souvenirs from Hell and Helloween: 4045 Patterson Lake Rd., Hell

COST: Free to visit; purchase prices vary.

PRO TIP: You can sign up to be mayor of Hell for one day. The cost is $100.

On the edge of Hell, you'll find the 11,000-acre Pinckney Recreation Area, a nature lover's paradise. Hiking, biking, swimming, canoeing, and kayaking on the Hell Chain of Lakes are all part of the fun.

The Gates of Hell

So, when the farmers heard that the taxman was coming to town, they would take the whiskey barrels from the general store's second floor, bring them down to the main floor, and take them to the dam. They would store the whiskey barrels underwater in the dam so they wouldn't have to pay taxes on the spirits. Once they received the word that the taxman had gone, they would retrieve the barrels and take them back up to the second level of the general store and continue to party.

Then, you find two alternatives to how the village became Hell. First, during harvest season, when someone inquired of the wives where their husbands were, they would reply, "He's gone to Hell." Another version is that when they asked Mr. Reeves what he wanted to name the hamlet, he replied, "I don't know! Name it Hell for all I care!" And so they did.

In any case, the name stuck, and Hell became an official town in 1841.

A LIGHT WITH WANDERLUST

Why is Tawas Point Lighthouse so far from the shores of Lake Huron?

Workers built the original lighthouse in 1853 in what was then known as Ottawa Point. With blowing and drifting sand, the predominant northeast wind resulted in a continually evolving endpoint that left the lighthouse so far from the endpoint that it was no longer effective.

In 1876, they built another lighthouse at the water's edge to remedy the situation. Workers used building materials from the abandoned lighthouse to fill the wooden crib surrounding the new lighthouse to protect it from the Great Lakes. The area continued to evolve, and by 1898, the lighthouse was once again surrounded by land. The point continues to change; today, the light stands approximately one mile from the point.

Eventually, they renamed Ottawa Point to Tawas Point. Located in East Tawas, Tawas Point Lighthouse is the only Victorian-era-style lighthouse on the Great Lakes, for those who love maritime history. The light features two colors—the red light marks the entrance to Tawas Bay 12 miles away, while the white light can be seen 12 miles into Lake Huron.

Take a lighthouse tour, learn about the era's keepers, and climb the tower to see a panoramic view of Lake Huron.

Birders enjoy this park in the spring and fall. It's a layover for migratory birds. You'll see hundreds, so you'll want your binoculars. Photographers will want their long lenses to get close-ups of birds in flight.

Tawas Point State Park is a little off the beaten path. Once you leave the expressway, you'll have about 30 miles on a two-lane highway before reaching your destination. But, during the drive, you'll have a chance to unwind. Once you get to the 183-acre state park on Tawas Bay, you'll find plenty to keep you busy. At the park, Lake Huron offers a sandy beach with warm, shallow water, perfect for swimming.

TAWAS POINT LIGHTHOUSE

WHAT: The Tawas Point Lighthouse is the only remaining example of a Victorian-era-style light station on the Great Lakes.

WHERE: Tawas Point State Park, 686 Tawas Beach Rd., East Tawas

COST: You need a Recreation Passport to enter the park: residents pay $13 annually; nonresidents pay $11 for a day pass, $39 annually.

PRO TIP: The state park offers a lighthouse keeper program. You can be a lighthouse keeper for a week during the summer. Responsibilities include providing tours of the former lighthouse keeper's quarters and the light tower.

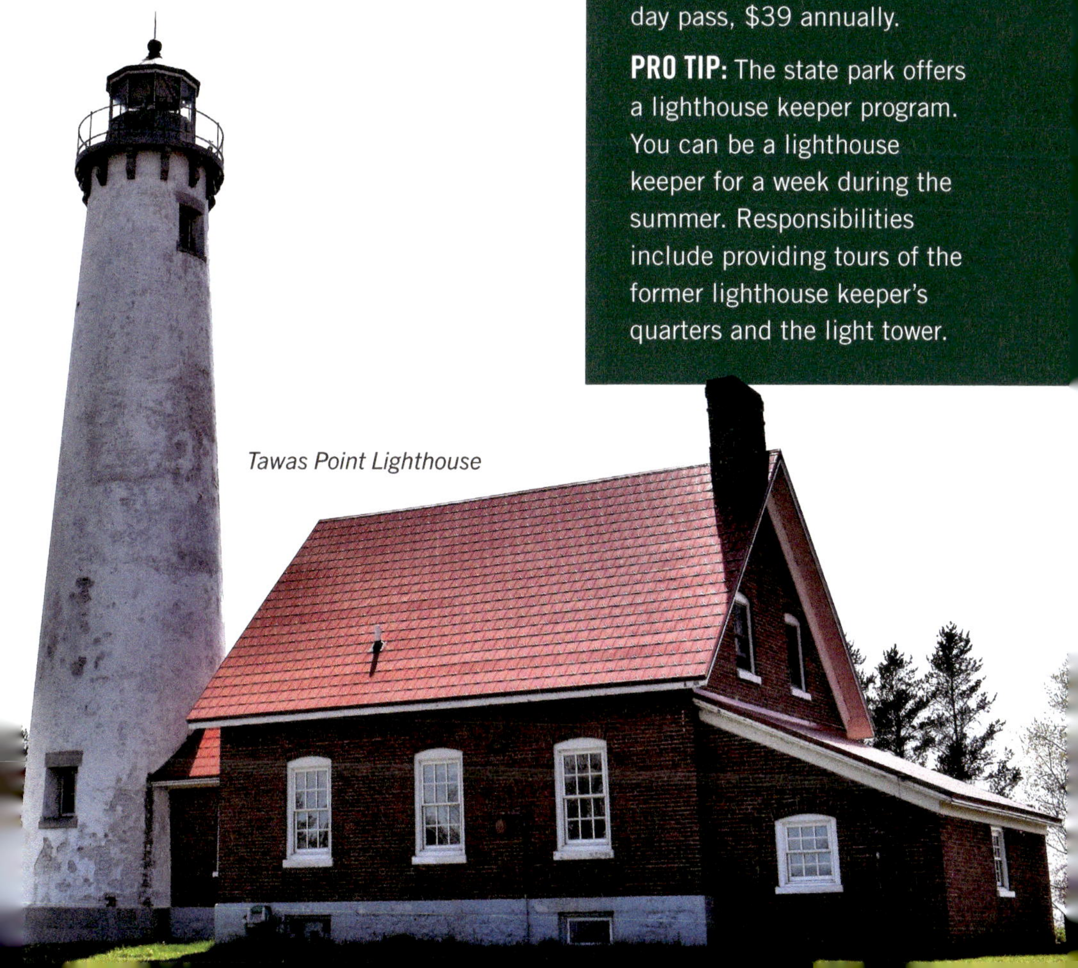

Tawas Point Lighthouse

A LEG UP

What's unique about the Legs Inn?

In Cross Village, the Legs Inn sits at the end of the M-119 Tunnel of Trees. The restaurant's name comes from the iron stove legs decorating its roofline. Legs Inn is a Michigan State Historic Site open seasonally from mid-May through mid-October.

Stanley Smolak, with the help of the Odawa (Ottawa) Indians, constructed the building with fieldstones on the outside and handcrafted wood on the inside. Smolak, a grassroots artist, used driftwood, tree limbs, and roots to carve furniture and decorative items, referring to them as nature's oddities.

They specialize in authentic Polish cuisine, so you'll find pierogi, Polish-style dumplings; kielbasa; golabki, cabbage rolls; and Polish smoked sausage with sauerkraut. You'll also find local Michigan favorites, like the smoked whitefish spread. Their house specialty combines cream cheese, smoked Great Lakes whitefish, and seasonings served with crackers and bread. Accompany those authentic Polish dishes with a draft beer.

This spot doesn't accept reservations, but if you arrive just as they open for lunch, you most likely won't wait more than a few minutes. Even though you may have to wait, browsing the on-site gift shop will quickly pass the time.

LEGS INN

WHAT: A Polish restaurant at the end of M-119's Tunnel of Trees

WHERE: 6425 N Lake Shore Dr., Cross Village

COST: The price of menu items varies depending on the meal selected.

PRO TIP: If you'd like to explore the area more, rent a cottage in Legs Inn's private wooded area, with sandy beach access to Lake Michigan.

Left: *White iron stove legs trim the roofline at Legs Inn.* Right: *Interior dining room at Legs Inn.*

If you prefer to eat on the patio, there is an outdoor dining garden with stunning views of Lake Michigan. Your wait may be over an hour, but the time will pass quickly in the outdoor waiting area, designed as a large grassy area with a garden and Adirondack chairs. You can get a drink from the bar and enjoy it in the garden, along with Lake Michigan's panoramic view. The space is so calming that you'll be sorry when your table is ready! Explore the waiting space behind the restaurant, even if there isn't a wait. The views of Lake Michigan are stunning from here.

Weekdays along the Tunnel of Trees are less busy than weekends. While the drive is only 20 miles long, take your time, make stops, and enjoy the journey.

IT'S NOT FREEZING

Why do two lakes and the connecting canal never freeze simultaneously?

In 1871, George Mitchell, a lumber baron, arrived in northern Michigan in search of lumber. He purchased and platted 2,000 acres of pine forest, which became Big Clam Village, today Cadillac.

For Mitchell to be successful, he had to convince the Grand Rapids & Indiana Railroad to change the destination of their railroad from Petoskey and Charlevoix to within a few miles of Little Clam Lake. Then, he had to dredge Black Creek, an easterly flowing waterway connecting the two lakes, to move lumber from the Big Clam Lake area to his lumber mills. His efforts failed, and the following year, he constructed the canal a few hundred feet south of Black Creek.

Mitchell originally built the man-made quarter-mile Clam Lake Canal, connecting Big Clam Lake and Little Clam Lake, to transfer logs between Little Clam Lake, now Lake Cadillac, and Big Clam Lake, now Lake Mitchell. In 1903, they changed all three names.

Clam Lake Canal is a picturesque spot that tourists and locals alike have always enjoyed, but it has been shrouded in a bit of mystery that many notice during winter. While the canal is still a tourist stop today, many have fun with it because of a mysterious winter occurrence. The lakes will freeze, and the channel will be open. Or the canal will be frozen, and the lakes won't—but the

---

William Mitchell State Park is a 660-acre park with boating, fishing, and camping. The Carl T. Johnson Hunting and Fishing Center at the park offers a variety of activities and displays, including a 500-gallon aquarium with fish from Lake Cadillac and Lake Mitchell.

Clam Lake Canal in winter. Photo courtesy of Cadillac Area Visitors Bureau

lakes and the channel never freeze simultaneously.

The logical explanation for the unusual occurrence is that the rapid water flow is the reason for the mysterious canal freezing while the lakes display open water. Shallow water freezes faster than deeper water, so the shoreline and waters freeze first. When the lakes freeze over, the canal opens for the remainder of winter, probably due to the swift current over its three- or four-foot depth.

Several decades ago, Robert Ripley's Believe It or Not! published the mystery of the Clam Lake Canal. Locals and visitors still discuss the phenomenon today.

CLAM LAKE CANAL

WHAT: A man-made canal connecting Lake Mitchell and Lake Cadillac

WHERE: 2506 North Blvd., Cadillac

COST: A Recreation Passport is required for Mitchell State Park; residents pay $13 annually; nonresidents pay $11 for a day pass, $39 annually.

PRO TIP: Starting at the Carl T. Johnson Hunting and Fishing Center, you'll find a 2.5-mile hiking loop that passes a lookout tower and fishing pier.

GNOME SWEET GNOME

Why did a builder only construct half a house?

Earl Young houses, also known as Mushroom Houses or Gnome Houses, are a collection of unique architectural structures in Charlevoix. Earl Young, a local builder and designer, was known for his whimsical, nature-inspired organic designs that integrated with the natural landscape. They blend into the surrounding landscape and resemble natural formations like mushrooms, gnome homes, or stone cottages.

While Earl Young built more than 25 unique residences and four commercial properties throughout his 50-year career, the buildings had several characteristics in common. Most Earl Young houses are seamlessly integrated with their natural surroundings, have low profiles almost hugging the ground, and roofs that are usually steeply pitched and covered with cedar shingles, adding to the rustic charm. Some homes feature rounded walls, curved lines, and unusual angles, resembling the organic shapes of nature.

Young constructed the houses primarily using locally sourced stone, including limestone, granite, and fieldstone. The rocks are typically irregularly shaped, making the structures look rugged and textured. The elaborate stonework on Earl Young's houses is highly intricate and skillfully crafted. The stones are carefully fitted together, often with little mortar, creating a visually appealing and durable structure.

The Half House gets its name for its unusual looks. It appears as if someone cut the house in half. But why did Young build half a house?

First, Young purchased the property at 300 Park Avenue and called it the Pines. He updated the existing home and used it as a rental property. Subsequently, he bought the neighboring property at 302 Park Avenue that once held the carriage house for the Pines.

Left: *The Half House on Front Street.*
Right: *The Green Mortar House showcasing the eyebrow dormer in the Boulder Subdivision.*

Soon after, the builder ran into an issue with the property lines. The city wouldn't allow Young to build beyond the property line, even though he owned both pieces of land. The result was an entire house that looked like half a house.

Young stopped short a few feet of the east property line and built a flat stucco slab chimney. The home has a tiny second-story bedroom, and from the rear, you can see a dormer window accent that adds light to the room. This house is one of the reasons Young's homes have been nicknamed gnome homes.

EARL YOUNG MUSHROOM HOUSES

WHAT: A group of more than 25 houses in Charlevoix built by Earl Young

WHERE: 302 Park Ave., Charlevoix

COST: Self-guided tours are free; you can download a map from visitcharlevoix.com or pick up one at the visitor center.

PRO TIP: These homes are privately owned and not open to the public. You can find some on vacation home rental sites if you want to stay overnight in an Earl Young home.

The GEM Car Tour provides a 50-minute guided tour of the Earl Young architecture in Charlevoix. The small-group tours offer opportunities to take pictures and ask questions.

BACK FROM THE BRINK

What measures did conservationists take to increase the numbers of these rare birds and remove them from the endangered species list?

Setophaga kirtlandii, once an endangered songbird commonly known as Kirtland's warbler, now has an increasing population in Michigan. While always a rare bird, their numbers began seriously declining in the 1960s. In the 10 years between 1961 and 1971, their numbers declined from 502 singing males to only 201. In the following decade, the annual census continued at around 200, with two counts as low as 167. In the 1990s, their numbers began to increase; by 2012, they hit approximately 2,000.

Two issues threatened these winged vocalists. First, they only breed in the young jack pine forests in north central Michigan and some parts of Ontario and Wisconsin. These trees grow in sandy soil and only have new growth after a fire. Kirtland's warblers only nest in a particular young tree between five feet to 25 feet tall, so a constant growth of new young trees is needed. The jack pine trees require fire to open their seed cones and begin new growth for young jack pine forests. Over the last 100 years, timber rotations and fire suppression reduced the Kirtland's warbler's habitat. To overcome this problem, conservationists used controlled burning to replenish the bird's habitat.

The second issue is the brown-headed cowbirds, which would take over the nests of the Kirtland's warblers, lay their eggs, and

---

Located in Grayling, Hartwick Pines State Park got its name from its 49 acres of old-growth pine forest, some of the last in Michigan. The park is one of the largest state parks in Michigan's Lower Peninsula.

Top: *Female Kirtland's warbler.* Bottom: *Male Kirtland's warbler. Photos courtesy of Michigan Audubon*

KIRTLAND'S WARBLERS

WHAT: The Kirtland's warbler, one of the rarest songbirds in North America

WHERE: The breeding area is on state-owned land where you'll find the jack pine habitat, located near Hartwick Pines State Park, 3612 State Park Dr., Grayling

COST: Tours are $15 per person. A Recreation Passport is required to enter Hartwick Pines State Park; residents pay $13 annually; nonresidents pay $11 for a day pass, $39 annually.

PRO TIP: You can take a self-guided car tour through the jack pine ecosystems, where you may see various wildlife, including the Kirtland's warbler. The 58-mile Jack Pine Wildlife Viewing Tour is marked with signs displaying Kirtland's warbler icons and watchable wildlife.

the Kirtland's eggs and young would perish. To resolve this issue, conservationists controlled the number of cowbirds, which resulted in fewer cowbirds parasitizing Kirtland's warblers' nests.

After being on the endangered species list for almost 50 years, the Kirtland's warbler's numbers increased to the point where, in October 2019, the birds were delisted. These yellow-breasted songbirds with gray topcoats leave Michigan in late summer to early fall to winter in the Bahamas.

BEYOND THE BADGE

How did nine cops save a 100-plus-year-old bakery from closing?

Clare City Bakery opened in 1896 when the town consisted of a grain elevator adjacent to the railroad tracks and a hardware store. The local farmers would go to town to visit the grain elevator, then stop by the bakery for a cuppa joe and a sweet treat. The doughnut shop and bakery have been in uninterrupted operation ever since.

But in 2009, the shop was within a few weeks of closing when the Clare Police Department heard the news. That's when the nine members of the local police department decided to take action to save the historic bakery. After a discussion about finances, all nine members of the police decided they were up for the challenge.

Historically, before patrol cars, the town had the beat cops who walked their area on foot. The only places open early in the morning were bakeries, where bakers encouraged the beat cops' presence to keep the less savory elements out of their business. Bakers invited cops to come in and provided coffee and doughnuts for their presence.

Today, Cops & Doughnuts is a destination tourist stop where 350,000 annual customers often arrive by the busload to eat doughnuts and participate in the fun wordplay. The shop has also brought customers to other businesses in the area, revitalizing downtown Clare.

In 2013, *Saveur* magazine named Cops & Doughnuts one of the finest doughnut shops in the United States and their Night Stick, a triple-chocolate long john, one of the best doughnuts in the world.

Left: *Entrance to Cops and Doughnuts.*
Right: *A box of doughnuts from Cops and Doughnuts in Clare.*

The shop has three sections. The first is a gift shop that sells T-shirts, hoodies, and other apparel with fun sayings like, "You have the right to remain glazed" or "D.W.I. Doughnuts Were Involved." The gift shop also sells Michigan food items like local honey and chocolate-covered cherries. The second area is the bakery case, brimming with various doughnuts named for anything related to the police, like the Night Stick, the Deputy, the Squeeler, and the Blue Goose—a reference to a patrol car. And finally, the third is a community gathering space to enjoy coffee and doughnuts and check out the mini museum.

COPS & DOUGHNUTS

WHAT: A cop-owned doughnut shop with award-winning doughnuts

WHERE: 521 N McEwan St., Clare

COST: Cost varies depending on purchases.

PRO TIP: Try the Driftwood, a long john stuffed with coconut cream and then topped with chocolate ganache and toasted coconut. The doughnut, which resembles a piece of driftwood, is the winner of the Cooking Channel's Donut Showdown competition.

LOST IN THE DEPTHS

What caused so many shipwrecks during the so-called "shipwreck century"?

Thunder Bay National Marine Sanctuary, next to Northwestern Lake Huron, is a 4,300-square-mile area that protects one of America's most nationally significant shipwreck groups. This area was one of the most dangerous water sections on the Great Lakes during the Shipwreck Century, the 100 years between 1825 and 1925. They often referred to the waters as Shipwreck Alley, which claimed about 200 ships in the Thunder Bay area. One hundred of those ships are still waiting to be discovered.

Several factors caused the large number of shipwrecks. First was the weather. Sixty-five percent of the wrecks during that time listed fog as the reason for an accident. During that period, weather predictions weren't reliable, and foghorns were the only technical assistance to avoid collisions and shipwrecks. It was often too late to react when a captain encountered an obstacle.

A second factor was the topography of Thunder Bay. The rocky shoreline and limestone reefs would cause holes in the

THUNDER BAY NATIONAL MARINE SANCTUARY

WHAT: Thunder Bay National Marine Sanctuary protects and preserves a collection of almost 100 nationally significant historic shipwrecks off the Michigan coast in Lake Huron.

WHERE: 500 W Fletcher St., Alpena

COST: Museum admission is free. Charges for Shipwreck Tours are adults, \$39; youth ages 6–12, \$14; ages 5 and under, \$1. Parking is free.

PRO TIP: When taking a tour, remain flexible in your tour times. Occasionally, tours must be rescheduled due to weather; however, the team may know a few days ahead and will contact you to advise.

Top: Lady Michigan, *a glass bottom boat used in viewing shipwrecks.* Inset: *A view of a shipwreck as seen through a glass bottom boat in Lake Huron.*

hulls of the ships. Again, without the technological advancements available today, it was impossible to avoid the inherent dangers of the shoreline.

The third factor was boat traffic. Within the shipwreck century, from 1869 to 1900, Michigan was the nation's largest producer of lumber. One of the significant ways to transport lumber was via Michigan's waterways, which resulted in even more shipwrecks.

In addition to the number of shipwrecks, what makes this nationally important is the wide variety of vessel types found at the Thunder Bay Marine Sanctuary. The wrecks include an 1844 sidewheel steamer and a 500-foot-long German freighter.

You don't have to be a diver to view these shipwrecks. Alpena Shipwreck Tours offers two-hour glass-bottom boat tours of Thunder Bay, where you can view shipwrecks from the boat.

FARM TO TABLE

How long does it take to become a chef?

Enrolling in Les Cheneaux Culinary School & Restaurant, where a nine-month culinary training program meets practical restaurant experience, culminates with real-life restaurant skills we all can enjoy. This upscale restaurant isn't big-city glitz and glam but the perfect combination of farm-to-table food in a maritime setting.

Nestled along the 12 miles of Lake Huron shoreline at the southeastern point of Michigan's Upper Peninsula, two coastal villages, Cedarville and Hessel, anchor the 36-island archipelago Les Cheneaux Islands. With just over 1,000 residents, the latter town is home to the Les Cheneaux Culinary School Restaurant.

They make everything from ketchup and mayonnaise to salad dressing and bread from scratch, using local ingredients where possible. They get their beef for the burgers from Mackinac Highland Beef, where the Scottish Highlander cattle are raised in St. Ignace in the winter and Rudyard in the summer. Their duck comes from Sugar Island, which is only accessed via ferry. The students learn to forage for components of their dishes. For example, in the spring, they'll look for Michigan favorites like morel mushrooms and ramps—a wild leek. Those ramps may be preserved through pickling for use later in the summer.

Sustainability is the cornerstone of their program. They even send compost scraps to local farmers to avoid waste.

The local theme continues with cocktails served using spirits from Les Cheneaux Distillers, an award-winning distiller in Cedarville. For that after-dinner coffee, the restaurant serves theirs from Les Cheneaux Coffee Roasters in Cedarville.

Left: *The kitchen at Les Cheneaux Culinary School Restaurant.* Right: *The view from the deck at Les Cheneaux.*

LES CHENEAUX CULINARY SCHOOL & RESTAURANT

WHAT: A farm-to-table restaurant where culinary students completing their internship are the chefs.

WHERE: 186 S Pickford Ave., Hessel

COST: Price varies depending upon menu selections.

PRO TIP: The restaurant serves dinner Wednesday through Sunday, mid-June through Labor Day.

The boathouse-themed decor features horizontal light wood paneling and light fixtures one would find on a northern Michigan boathouse. Black-and-white photos from circa the 1950s adorn the walls.

In addition to dining inside, you'll find a covered deck with views of Hessel Bay to experience the Michigan outdoors. Seating on the lower deck is the perfect place to have a glass of Michigan wine or a craft cocktail. The indoor-outdoor bar area makes it easy to grab one more drink while remaining outside.

While the menu is laser focused, you won't feel limited in your selections. Even with the small menu, the variety ranges from upscale choices typically found in fine-dining restaurants to casual pub-style items like soft pretzels and hamburgers. So, no matter the style of food you're in the mood for, there'll be something you'll enjoy.

DIGGING DEEP

Where is one of North America's longest ongoing archaeological digs, and what are they uncovering?

French soldiers constructed Fort Michilimackinac in 1715 as a fur-trading outpost. The French fort played a crucial role in the North American fur trade, serving as a hub for French traders and engaging in commerce with Native American tribes.

During the mid-18th century, the fort became a center of contention between the French and the British during the French and Indian War. In 1761, British forces under the command of Captain George Etherington captured the fort from the French without any resistance. This marked a shift in control, and Michilimackinac and other French territories were yielded to the British under the Treaty of Paris.

The British moved Fort Michilimackinac to Mackinac Island. In 1780, during the American Revolutionary War, the British relocated the fort from the mainland to Mackinac Island to better control the region's strategic waterway. The move was also motivated because the mainland fort had been vulnerable to attacks by Native American tribes allied with the American rebels. The British constructed a new fort on Mackinac Island, known as Fort Mackinac, which became an important military outpost in

COLONIAL MICHILIMACKINAC

WHAT: A reconstructed fort built on the original site, active archaeological excavations, and a museum containing finds from the digs

WHERE: 102 W Straits Ave., Mackinaw City

COST: Adults, $14.50; youth ages 5–12, $8.75; under 5, free. Parking is free.

PRO TIP: Get a map and schedule of the day's events at the visitors center, and plan to spend between two and four hours at the fort.

the Great Lakes region. What they didn't move, they burned to the ground. Eventually, blowing sand covered the area.

The Michilimackinac archaeological excavation began in 1959 and has continued every summer from early June until mid-August. Archaeologists have recovered over one million artifacts since the dig began, with approximately 65 percent of the fort being excavated to date. Archaeologists at the dig site are available to answer questions while they work.

An exhibit, *Treasures from the Sand*, showcases hundreds of archaeologically excavated artifacts from Colonial Michilimackinac.

Today, Colonial Michilimackinac is a National Historic Landmark that features 13 reconstructed buildings with period furnishings, interactive exhibits, and demonstrations.

Colonial Michilimackinac offers excellent up-close views of the Mackinac Bridge.

Colonial Michilimackinac

THE STEEL CHRONICLES

Why is there a Mackinaw Bridge Museum above an Italian restaurant?

The majestic five-mile suspension bridge, the Mighty Mac, spans Michigan's Upper and Lower Peninsulas. The Original Mackinaw Bridge Museum, sitting above MaMa Mia's Pizzeria and Restaurant, pays tribute to the ironworkers who built this phenomenal construction.

J. C. Stilwell, the restaurant's owner, was one of the ironworkers who built the Mackinac Bridge and ultimately created the museum. Stilwell married a woman of Italian heritage from East Detroit, hence the origins of the Italian restaurant.

Stilwell bought a spinning wheel used to build the massive Mackinac Bridge cables and a movie that told the story of the bridge's construction. These purchases were the beginning of the museum. Soon, ironworkers from around the nation began donating artifacts to the museum. Tools and parts used to build the bridge—along with photographs, documents, and even a diving suit—poured into what eventually became the museum.

On August 28, 2005, an early Sunday morning, a fire started in a storage area near the museum. One hundred firefighters from seven fire departments helped fight the fire. But, five hours later, the fire had destroyed the Original Mackinaw Bridge Museum and MaMa Mia's Pizzeria and Restaurant.

The fire didn't deter Stilwell He rebuilt and reopened his museum and restaurant in 2007. In the process, hundreds of people who had enjoyed the previous museum donated their

---

The family-owned-and-operated MaMa Mia's Pizzeria and Restaurant serves award-winning pizza.

A tribute to iron workers inside the museum

THE MACKINAW BRIDGE MUSEUM

WHAT: A museum with exhibits about the Mackinac Bridge construction

WHERE: 231 E Central Ave., Mackinaw City

COST: Museum admission is free.

PRO TIP: Order a pizza at the counter-style restaurant and explore the museum while you wait for your food.

family-owned artifacts to the new museum. While J. C. Stilwell passed away on January 26, 2013, the museum continues his legacy.

Today, the museum pays homage to the five men—three ironworkers, a laborer, and a diver—who lost their lives during the construction of the Mighty Mac. You'll find several movies on continuous loops throughout the museum, including one in a theater-style setting. These movies tell the tales from different perspectives of working on the Mighty Mac. Hard hats and news articles contribute to the stories.

The museum is open during restaurant hours, spring through fall.

INTO THE WILD

Where and when are the best elk-viewing opportunities?

By the late 1880s, habitat issues and overhunting eliminated Michigan's native elk population. In 1918, the state transferred seven Rocky Mountain elk to northern Michigan. Today, from those seven animals, Michigan is home to more than 1,000 elk, one of largest free-range elk herds east of the Mississippi. The Department of Natural Resources cares for the forest and wildlife through careful management, which allows the elk to flourish in the Pigeon River Country's 114,000-acre state forest.

While the elk live in the area year-round, you'll have a better chance of seeing them in September and October or April and May due to their activity levels. In the fall, the males establish their mating rights and are active with bugling and using their antlers to break brush. These activities intimidate their rivals and impress the female elk. It is better to plan to view elk midweek this time of year, as weekends have become crowded.

GAYLORD'S CITY ELK PARK

WHAT: The City of Gaylord supports an elk herd with public viewing areas, where you will be almost sure to see elk.

WHERE: The Elks Lodge, 116 Grandview Blvd., Gaylord

COST: Free

PRO TIP: Take binoculars or long lenses to improve viewing opportunities.

In northern Michigan, cell service and GPS devices may be unreliable. You'll find maps for other elk viewing areas at the Gaylord Tourism Bureau Information Center or the Pigeon River Country State Forest Headquarters.

An elk at Gaylord's City Elk Park in fall. Photo courtesy of Elizabeth Olney

In late April and early May, elk are active, eating the green growth of spring. Fewer people are out viewing during this time, so it is an excellent time to look for elk. Fall is the most photographic time of year to view elk, with their enormous antlers and fall colors in the background. In the spring, the male elk lose their antlers.

Here are some places where you're likely to spot elk:

- East Sturgeon Valley Road, about eight miles east of Vanderbilt, where you'll see a DNR-signed elk-viewing area
- A cleared parking lot and field three miles north of Sturgeon Valley Road on Fontinalis Road
- About one-half mile north of the intersection of Clark Bridge Road and Osmun Road

NATURE'S SCULPTURE

What are the best ways to get a glimpse of Turnip Rock?

Situated on the eastern coast of Michigan's Lower Peninsula, near the tip of the Thumb region, Turnip Rock rises 50 feet above the crystal-clear waters of Lake Huron. The lake's constant waves striking against the limestone over millions of years created an awe-inspiring geological formation. A slender, vertical column resembling a giant turnip's root, with the trees sprouting from the top resembling the turnip's top, inspired the whimsical name.

Since the Pointe Aux Barques cottage community owns the land, the rock is considered private and accessible only by water. Visitors must venture out onto the waters of Lake Huron to see it. Paddling is the most frequent means of seeing the rock. The trip by kayak or canoe is approximately seven miles round trip and takes two to four hours of paddling in a northeast direction along the shallow shoreline. Planning your visit during calm weather is essential to ensure a safe and enjoyable experience. If it is windy or Lake Huron has waves, you should wait until another day. South winds can push paddlers so far onto Lake Huron that a rescue may be necessary.

TURNIP ROCK

WHAT: One of Michigan's natural wonders

WHERE: 329R+89, Port Austin

COST: Free

PRO TIP: Even if you don't plan to rent a kayak, stop by Port Austin Kayak Rentals for weather conditions and maps.

If you aren't up for the physical challenges of kayaking to Turnip Rock, you can also see it through one of the local boat tour companies.

Top: *Turnip Rock at sunset.* Inset: *Turnip Rock on Lake Huron. Photos courtesy of Turnip Rock Tours LLC*

You'll want to come prepared for the trip with life jackets, sunscreen, sunglasses, snacks, and water bottles. Rental facilities and guided tours that cater to all experience levels are available in the nearby town of Port Austin. As you navigate the pristine waters, watch for various wildlife species, such as bald eagles and Great Lakes fish. Take your camera to capture the fantastic views at sunrise or sunset, when the sun's warm glow accentuates the rock's natural beauty.

THE FLAVOR OF HISTORY

How did Rosen rye reemerge on South Manitou Island?

Mammoth Distilling is a craft distillery based near Central Lake, committed to using local ingredients. They strive to showcase the flavors and characteristics of Michigan by using locally grown grains and botanicals in their products.

In 2019, Mammoth Distilling embarked on an extraordinary journey. They sought to obtain certified Rosen rye seed—from the USDA seed bank in Colorado. This heritage seed would be the foundation for their ambitious plan to establish a Rosen rye seed farm on South Manitou Island.

The same year, Mammoth Distilling collaborated with Michigan State University's AgBioResearch. Within the university's state-of-the-art facilities, large walk-in coolers, and isolated greenhouses, they successfully propagated multiple cycles of Rosen rye. This meticulous process enabled them to produce a certified seed supply, marking the start of their foundation crop.

In 2020, Mammoth Distilling achieved another milestone. With the assistance of Michigan State University, Empire

---

Manitou Island Transit provides horse-drawn wagon tours of South Manitou Island. One tour includes the Hutzler Farm, the Beck Farm, and the old schoolhouse. The other consists of the Valley of the Giants and the wreck of the *Francisco Morazan*. If you are going on a day trip to South Manitou Island, you will only have enough time for one tour.

Mammoth Distilling Tasting Room in Traverse City

Malting Company, and a special use permit from the National Park Service, Mammoth Distilling sowed the foundation crop on Hutzler Farm using hand tools. This was significant because it was the first time Rosen rye had been planted on South Manitou Island since 1950.

Then, in 2021, Mammoth Distilling's efforts bore fruit. For the first time in over 70 years, a crop of Rosen rye grown on South Manitou Island was certified. With the certification, Mammoth Distilling set its sights on a grander scale. In 2022, they planned to distribute the seeds to mainland farmers, allowing them to cultivate their own distillation stock. The revival of Rosen rye would spread beyond South Manitou Island as farmers across the mainland eagerly anticipated the opportunity to participate in this historical renaissance.

And so, Mammoth Distilling's journey to revive Rosen Rye reached a pivotal moment. Through their unwavering dedication, collaboration, and the resilience of nature, the once-forgotten grain found new life.

MAMMOTH DISTILLING

WHAT: Mammoth Distilling is a craft distillery that has begun growing Rosen rye once again on South Manitou Island.

WHERE: 2407 Main St., Central Lake, is the original location. You'll find Mammoth Distilling tasting rooms throughout northern Michigan.

COST: Varies depending on purchase

PRO TIP: Call ahead to take a guided tour of their distillery. The tour provides insights into their distillation process, the history of their spirits, and other interesting details you may not discover on your own.

Prehistoric Super Salamander

PREHISTORIC PARADISE

How did two dozen dinosaurs become a family roadside attraction?

Paul Nathan Domke was born to Prussian immigrants on December 31, 1886, in Presque Isle County. He joined the United States Navy in 1906, working in various hospital roles worldwide. In 1910, he left the navy and returned to his family farm in northern Michigan. He moved to Rogers City and then to Detroit, where he worked as a church decorator.

During his military service, Domke became interested in natural history, mainly extinct creatures. When his painting and decorating business failed during the Great Depression, he and his wife returned to northern Michigan and bought land near Ossineke. In 1930, Domke built his home, several rental cabins, a gas station, and an art studio.

While he went to museums and saw dinosaur bones, he thought it would be fun to see life-size dinosaurs with muscle and skin, as they might have looked when dinosaurs roamed the earth. In 1935, he began building the first displays that would become Dinosaur Gardens. Initially, he used plaster of Paris and other materials, but the dinosaurs didn't stand up to the weather. With the help of a local chemist, Domke eventually developed a durable cement mixture. Each creature required a concrete foundation and a steel framework to support the sculpted details. He created a pliable cement plastic made from cement, animal hair, and asphalt.

Future paleontologists can gain some experience by participating in one of the fossil dig activities. They can comb through real dinosaur fossils and keep their favorite three fossils.

Domke took great care in researching and constructing each animal in his prehistoric zoo, ensuring that they were accurately sized and resembled their appearances when they roamed the earth. He studied at the Smithsonian Institution and toured locations in Canada to gather accurate information.

Over nearly 40 years, from 1935 to 1967, Domke created a zoo consisting of about 27 prehistoric creatures. In 1960, Frank McCourt and his wife, Wilma, purchased the property during construction. Wilma sold the zoo on a land contract in 1980 but regained ownership shortly after. Frank and Judy, Wilma's son and daughter-in-law, added their contributions to the park, including a mini-golf course and a dinosaur sculpture created by another artist.

Velociraptor

In 2013, Gary and Connie Stephan, owners of Connie's Cafe, acquired Dinosaur Gardens. They renovated the gift shop, added an ice cream shop with a wide range of toppings, and continued maintaining the park. Walking through the garden, you can imagine the prehistoric sea that once covered the land.

Dinosaur Gardens showcases creatures from various periods, spanning over 200 million to 34 million years ago. Visitors can take a half-mile walk around the fern-covered property to witness the incredible animals firsthand and transport themselves to the time of the dinosaurs.

DINOSAUR GARDENS

WHAT: A roadside attraction consisting of a zoo containing more than 25 prehistoric creatures, a Putt-Putt golf course, an ice cream shop, and a café.

WHERE: 11160 US Hwy. 23 S, Ossineke

COST: Adults: walking tour, $10; Putt-Putt golf, $6. Children under 3, free. A variety of packaged bundles are available.

PRO TIP: Dinosaur Gardens is a seasonal venue, open Memorial Day through Labor Day.

A FERRY TALE

What ship is a designated continuation of a United States highway?

The SS *Badger*, a National Historic Landmark, is the last coal-fired steamship in the United States. Built in Sturgeon Bay, Wisconsin, she got her name from the University of Wisconsin Badgers. The 410-foot ship began operating in 1953 and can hold 600 passengers and 180 vehicles. Engineers designed the boat to carry railroad cars across Lake Michigan year-round. They engineered and reinforced the hull specifically to break the ice. She can manage almost any Lake Michigan weather.

The 565-mile-long US Highway 10 begins in Bay City, Michigan, and ends in Fargo, North Dakota, ultimately spanning four states. The only interruption is Lake Michigan, one of the Great Lakes. In 2015, officials named the SS *Badger* a designated continuation of US Highway 10. The ship is one of only two ferry systems connecting the nation's highways. The other is US Route 9.

Since engineers designed the ship initially to carry railroad cars across Lake Michigan, she has no problems carrying other oversized loads, like motor coaches, semitrucks, and farming equipment. In 2022, the SS *Badger* also became an official federal

SS *BADGER*

WHAT: The last coal-fired steamship in the United States

WHERE: 701 Maritime Dr., Ludington

COST: Summer round-trip prices: adults, $155; seniors 65+, $141; college students, $141; active military, $141; children (ages 5–15), $76; children 4 and under, free; autos, vans, SUVs, pickup trucks, $167. Parking at both sites is free. Other pricing varies.

PRO TIP: Ludington is in the Eastern Time Zone (ET), while Manitowoc is in the Central Time Zone (CT).

Top: Badger *angled with the sun. Photo courtesy of SpeedShot Ship Photography.* Inset: *Museum on-board the SS* Badger *car ferry. Photo courtesy of Lake Michigan Carferry*

marine highway, where not only tourists ride but also freight trucks, along with cars, motorcycles, bicycles, vans, SUVs, pickup trucks, RVs, and campers. This route reduces traffic on busy highways around Chicago while reducing the carbon footprint.

The steamship makes the four-hour trip across Lake Michigan daily from Ludington, Michigan, to Manitowoc, Wisconsin. But the time will pass quickly with all the activities you can do onboard. In addition to playing free Badger Bingo, with prizes, you can have a meal overlooking the water, watch a movie in the free theater, or shop.

Plan to disconnect on your journey across Lake Michigan, as you won't find cell towers in the middle of Lake Michigan. However, you can buy Wi-Fi on board.

BIG SPRING, BIGGER MARVEL

Where can you take a raft to the middle of a spring without fear of drifting off course?

This treasure, tucked away in Palms Book State Park, is Michigan's largest spring, Kitch-iti-kipi. Translated as "the big spring," it is one of those beautiful spots you'll be sorry you missed if you don't stop. The park began at the turn of the last century, when John Bellaire, the owner of the Five and Dime in Manistique, made arrangements with the Palms Book Lumber Company to purchase the initial 90 acres that made up the park for $10. Today, the park has grown to about 388 acres.

The pool is 200 feet across and 40 feet deep with a stunning emerald-green bottom. Over 10,000 gallons of crystal-clear water gushes from the cracks in the spring's underlying limestone every minute. With a water temperature of 45 degrees Fahrenheit year-round, the spring doesn't freeze.

A complimentary, self-propelled group raft with a center opening allows a closer look at the trout at the bottom of the spring. You'll find the raft attached to a pulley system that spans the mouth of the spring so that you can turn a crank and stop and start at the exact place you want to view the spring.

KITCHI-ITI-KIPI

WHAT: Michigan's largest freshwater spring

WHERE: Approximately 11 miles off Hwy. 2 at the north end of M-149, a mile north of County Rd. 455 Junction, Manistique

COST: A Recreation Passport is required for Palms Book State Park: residents pay $13 annually; nonresidents pay $11 for a day pass, $39 annually.

PRO TIP: The trail leading to the observation raft and the raft itself are both ADA accessible.

Kitch-iti-Kipi, Michigan's largest spring at Palms Book State Park

The water is so clear you might think you're viewing the fish in a swimming pool. Native Americans have called Kitch-iti-kipi the "Mirror to Heaven," as the aquamarine and emerald pool reflects the surrounding forest.

Palms Book State Park is a year-round, day-use park offering modern restrooms, a picnic area, a concession, and a park store.

ROOTED IN BEAUTY

Who donned the green cape and became the hero of the Tunnel of Trees, preserving its beauty for generations to come?

Michigan 119 (M-119) twists along Lake Michigan's shoreline with short twists and hairpin curves. The Scenic Heritage Route stands out as one of the narrowest highways in the country, lacking both shoulders and a centerline. The hardwoods grow at the road's edge, with their leafy canopies stretching over the highway, creating an experience similar to going through a tunnel.

In 1936, Alice Irwin employed her statewide newspaper column to create a grassroots effort to protect and preserve the trees lining M-119, now known as the Tunnel of Trees. Recognizing the importance of this scenic stretch, she advocated for its preservation and rallied local organizations and residents to join the cause. She shared stories about the trees' history, ecological importance, and cultural significance to the region through her column. Irwin's efforts aimed to generate public support and safeguard the Tunnel of Trees from threats such as road expansion or development.

Apart from its aesthetic appeal, the Tunnel of Trees serves a vital ecological role. The trees play a crucial part in preserving the bluffs of the area. Their roots anchor the soil, aiding in soil retention, while their growth enhances water absorption, replenishing the groundwater that nourishes Lake Michigan and mitigating the risk of flooding. Additionally, the foliage acts as a natural shield, reducing the impact of rainfall on exposed surfaces and minimizing erosion.

While the highway spans a mere 20.5 miles, and you can drive it in approximately an hour, make some stops along the way. Highway markers strategically placed along the route offer insights into the historical background of the tunnel, adding to the overall experience of exploration and discovery.

Left: *M-119, the scenic heritage root known as the Tunnel of Trees.* Right: *M-119 Tunnel of Trees Scenic Byway sign.*

Today, the Tunnel of Trees remains an iconic and cherished landmark in Michigan, attracting tourists from far and wide who experience its breathtaking beauty and serenity. The success of preserving this scenic drive is due partially to the initial efforts and vision of Alice Irwin, who recognized its value and worked to ensure its preservation for future generations.

TUNNEL OF TREES

WHAT: M-119, the Tunnel of Trees, is a scenic drive beginning in Harbor Springs known for its picturesque canopy.

WHERE: M-119 begins in Harbor Springs and ends in Cross Village.

COST: Free

PRO TIP: You'll find significantly fewer crowds during the week along the Tunnel of Trees than on weekends.

As you make your way along M-119, stop at Pond Hill Farms near Harbor Springs. The farm includes year-round fun for the entire family. You'll find everything from a winery and brewery to hayrides, a giant pumpkin patch, cider and doughnuts, and live music.

PETRIFIED PERFECTION

What is a Petoskey stone, and where can you find one?

A Petoskey stone is a distinctive fossilized coral scientifically known as *Hexagonaria percarinata.* This stone showcases intricate patterns of honeycomb-shaped cells on its surface, creating a stunning mosaic reminiscent of ancient marine life. With hues ranging from pale gray to warm beige, this stone is a testament to the rich geological history of the Great Lakes region.

You'll find Petoskey stones along the shores of Lake Michigan, particularly in the northern part of the state. Beaches such as Magnus Park, Petoskey State Park, Charlevoix, and Elk Rapids are renowned for their abundance of these natural treasures. Additionally, areas with exposed Devonian-age limestone, such as the Alpena and Traverse City regions, may yield Petoskey stones. With 1,000 feet of rocky shoreline, Magnus Park offers one of the best places to find Michigan's sought-after state stone.

PETOSKEY STONES

WHAT: Michigan's state stone, which is fossilized coral

WHERE: 2475 M-119 Hwy., Petoskey

COST: Free

PRO TIP: Be aware of state or federal regulations when hunting rocks. The Michigan DNR states you can only remove 25 pounds of stones annually.

If you'd like to try polishing your Petoskey stones, stop by NorthGoods in Petoskey to purchase a polishing kit. If your hunt for the state stone wasn't successful, or you want a polished stone that shows off the pattern, check out Grandpa Shorter's Gifts, also in Petoskey.

Petoskey State Park's beach is sandier, but Petoskey stones are still simple to find.

Polished Petoskey stones

Tips for finding Petoskey stones:

- Plan your search during low tide or after storms when the waves have brought fresh stones ashore, increasing your chances of finding them.
- Hunting for Petoskey stones is a delightful but sometimes challenging endeavor. Be patient, explore different areas, and enjoy the process of discovering these natural treasures.
- Petoskey stones have unique hexagonal patterns that resemble honeycombs. Scan the shoreline for rocks with these distinct markings.
- While most Petoskey stones are gray or beige, watch for subtle hints of pink, lavender, or green. These color variations add an extra touch of rarity to your collection.
- Wetting a Petoskey stone can enhance its patterns and make them more visible. Carry a spray bottle when hunting for Petoskey stones, as wet rocks are easier to find.

The Petoskey stone is more than just a fossil; it symbolizes Michigan's geological heritage. With its intricate patterns and rich history, finding a Petoskey stone along the shores of Lake Michigan is a rewarding experience. So, next time you're wandering the beaches of Michigan, keep your eyes peeled, let the waves guide you, and uncover the beauty of these ancient treasures. Happy hunting!

A Petoskey stone on the beach

MY HANDS ARE CLEAN

What peculiar museum resides within a Michigan State University employee's office?

John French, an employee at Michigan State University, turned his office at the university's planetarium into an unusual museum. French has collected moist towelettes from around the world, many through donations.

One of the most fascinating towelettes is Finger Pinkies, advertised as "the secretary's hand cleaner." In the 21st century, it's difficult to imagine how a secretary's hands might become so dirty at her desk to require a hand cleaner. But rewind several decades, and the reverse side of the packet reminds us that typewriter ribbon ink, carbon paper, money, and newspapers all dirtied a secretary's hands.

THE MOIST TOWELETTE MUSEUM

WHAT: A museum dedicated to moist towelettes

WHERE: Inside Abrams Planetarium, Michigan State University, 755 Science Rd., Room 100, East Lansing

COST: Free

PRO TIP: Open Monday through Friday, 9 a.m. to noon and 1 p.m. to 4:30 p.m. Note they close over lunch hour.

Other interesting towelettes include a group of *Star Trek*–themed packages from the original show, those from Hard Rock Cafes around the world, and health-related wipes, like the MammoWipe.

One sample stands out among the unopened towelettes—the only used towelette in the museum. Where did it come from? None other than Tom and Ray Magliozzi, the hosts from the radio program *Car Talk*. While French requested them to donate any towelette they had, he had no idea they would send him one they had used. After

Left: *The Moist Towelette Museum.* Right: *The museum's curator John French holds the only used towelette in the museum.*

careful consideration, he decided not to ask other celebrities for their used towelettes because he thought it would be "a little weird."

While Moist Towelette Museum's website provides a sampling of the towelettes contained in the museum, you'll need to visit to thoroughly understand the massive variation in the number of moist towelettes.

As an outreach program from the Department of Physics and Astronomy, the Talbert and Leota Abrams Planetarium, located on the campus of Michigan State University, is an astronomy and space education resource center for central Michigan.

LOST WITH THE LUMBER

What happened to the lumber town of Singapore?

Often referred to as Michigan's Pompeii, land speculators established Singapore in 1837 near the mouth of the Kalamazoo River. In the early 1800s, where today dunes tower high above the ground, the land was flat and covered in white pines, Michigan's state tree. Time and wind have erased all evidence of what was once one of Michigan's most prosperous towns.

The town was a lumbering community on the Great Lakes where forestry was the town's wealth. When the city was booming, several hundred people lived and worked there, with three mills, a bank, and two hotels. The town was on track to become the next big town on Lake Michigan.

In 1871, the Great Chicago Fire changed everything. Singapore was positioned across Lake Michigan from Chicago and in a perfect position to supply building materials. Singapore

SINGAPORE, MICHIGAN

WHAT: A lost city that stood approximately two miles north of where Saugatuck stands today

WHERE: 102 Butler St., Saugatuck, is where Singapore's Michigan historical marker stands.

COST: Free to visit Saugatuck. Saugatuck Dune Rides are adults, $25; children ages 3–11, $15; children 2 and under, free.

PRO TIP: A Saugatuck Dune Rides Tour is a great way to learn more about the history of Singapore and the Lake Michigan dunes.

Singapore's bank, which now stands in Saugatuck, printed its own money. Today, the bank is known for having elaborately decorated banknotes.

Left: *Singapore buried beneath the sand.* Right: *A Singapore historic marker at Saugatuck Village Hall.*

exported six million feet of lumber to assist with Chicago's rebuild. Within 10 years, they cut down all the trees, and the town went from prosperous to impoverished. People began to relocate from Singapore. Ultimately, the town dismantled the mills, and they moved many buildings into downtown Saugatuck.

The townspeople never planted any additional trees, resulting in further problems. Strong winds against the sand eventually buried what remained of Singapore. For 85 years, the dunes were moving at 10 feet per year. Today, it's a lost town that vanished without a trace beneath Lake Michigan's dunes.

FROM CRISIS TO CONSERVATION

How did the Civilian Conservation Corps contribute to Michigan's reforestation efforts?

The Higgins Lake Nursery began in 1903 as an experiment in reforestation. In 1903, a team under the direction of State Forest Warden Filibert Roth reviewed the land covered largely in stumps and sand on the north shore of Higgins Lake. What was once a flourishing forest was now desecrated from aggressive lumbering and several 19th-century fires.

The Michigan Legislature created the Michigan Forestry Commission to tackle the problem. Their mission was to replant trees and create Michigan's first forest service and tree nursery. By 1904, over 600,000 seedlings were growing; by 1906, the team had developed 27 tree species. By 1926, the nursery distributed 22 million seedlings throughout the country.

President Franklin D. Roosevelt began the Civilian Conservation Corps (CCC) during the Great Depression, employing primarily young men ages 17 to 23 in many public works projects. In Michigan, thousands of men fought forest fires and planted trees across northern Michigan.

By the 1930s, more than 100,000 men joined the federal Depression-era Civilian Conservation Corps and completed decades of work in only nine years. In 1933, the Higgins Lake CCC Camp began working at the nursery.

The 1,364-acre South Higgins Lake State Park is known for its various water recreation offerings. Spring-fed Higgins Lake is clear and features boating and fishing opportunities.

Higgins Lake State Park and Nursery where you'll find the CCC Museum.

By the time the CCC program ended in 1942, workers had planted 484 million trees, two times greater than any other state. At the beginning of the 1960s, the initial reforestation efforts were almost complete, and the Higgins Lake Nursery closed.

It ultimately became one of the world's largest pines nurseries and was the basis for creating a successful state forest system. Today, Michigan features stunning forests.

HIGGINS LAKE NURSERY AND CCC MUSEUM

WHAT: A museum dedicated to the role of the Civilian Conservation Corps in reforesting Michigan

WHERE: 11747 N Higgins Lake Dr., Roscommon

COST: Admission to the museum is free, but a Recreation Passport is required for Higgins Lake State Park; residents pay $13 annually; nonresidents pay $11 for a day pass, $39 annually.

PRO TIP: The nursery area and CCC Museum only have vault toilets. Modern restrooms are available at the campground.

QUILLS AND THRILLS

How did the Porcupine Mountains get their name?

Early explorers thought the forested crests of Porcupine Mountains Wilderness State Park resembled porcupine quills. Located in Ontonagon County, at the west end of Michigan's Upper Peninsula, the area became known as the Porcupine Mountains or, as locals lovingly refer to it, the Porkies.

Porcupine Mountains Wilderness State Park offers many year-round outdoor activities. You can explore more than 90 miles of hiking trails, one of the park's most popular activities. Chasing waterfalls gives hiking a purpose. You'll also experience panoramic views from the overlooks, like Lake of the Clouds and Summit Peak.

You'll find an ADA-accessible walkway and wooden ramp from the parking lot to the Lake of the Clouds observation area. With benches at regular intervals along the walkway, it's an easy 300 feet. In contrast, the entire trail is a 1.4-mile out-and-back. The over-60,000-acre park features North America's largest tract of virgin hardwoods. Visit the Lake of the Clouds in late September through the first week in October to experience the stunning amber,

PORCUPINE MOUNTAIN WILDERNESS STATE PARK

WHAT: Michigan's largest and arguably most beautiful state park

WHERE: 33303 Headquarters Rd., Ontonagon

COST: A Recreation Passport is required for Porcupine Mountain Wilderness State Park; residents pay $13 annually; nonresidents pay $11 for a day pass, $39 annually.

PRO TIP: EnChroma-enabled viewers offer those who are colorblind a way to view a complete range of colors at Lake of the Clouds scenic overlook, Nawadaha Falls, and Summit Peak Observation Tower.

orange, and crimson fall foliage. You're high above the trees from the overlook, and the color explodes.

The park has more than 90 waterfalls, some off the beaten track, while others are easy to reach. Agate Falls and Bond Falls are two favorites. Agate Falls, one of Michigan's most scenic, is a succession of falls with a 40-foot drop over a ledge of terraced sandstone. Bond Falls, a natural waterfall improved by a dam, features a 50-foot drop with several smaller cascades.

Open from mid-May until mid-October, the visitors center is great for familiarizing yourself with the park. If you're a hiker, you can sign up for interpretive hikes, check on trail conditions, get directions, and pick up your backcountry camping permits. Seasonal roads close from the beginning of December until late spring. That said, you can access the area via snowmobile and cross-country skiing during the winter.

The first music festival held in a Michigan state park was the Porcupine Mountains Music Festival. The event happens the weekend before Labor Day, where they have a variety of live music, including rock, bluegrass, country, Americana, blues, and folk. Check their website for this year's schedule.

Lake of the Clouds in the Porcupine Mountains

HISTORY MEETS HOSPITALITY

What made Kate Cartier as modern as her mansion?

Warren and Kate Cartier built their three-story neoclassical home in 1905. They trimmed the Roman-pressed brick with Bedford limestone. Fitting for a lumber baron, the interior features different types of wood in each room—including mahogany, oak, cherry, walnut, and maple. The Cartier Mansion Bed and Breakfast is listed on the National Register of Historic Places today.

The Cartiers wintered in Fort Myers, Florida, where their circle of friends included Henry Ford, Harvey Firestone, and Thomas Edison. Warren got some of his home inspiration from Edison, who encouraged the Cartiers to be early adopters of electronic devices and modern technology. At that time, only 3 percent of the homes in the United States had electricity. The light fixtures in the Cartier mansion were double-plumbed for both electricity and gas. They made gas to power the lights in the home's basement. Today, the mansion even has the original light fixtures.

Kate loved to throw parties, so the dining room offered features to make entertaining more efficient. A button hidden in the floor allowed for a subtle call to staff. The ornate radiator concealed a warming oven beside the built-in sycamore wood buffet.

The Edison Suite is now in the carriage house where Kate parked her 1917 Detroit Electric car—purchased without Warren's knowledge, a bold move for a woman of the early

---

You can see Kate Cartier's 1917 Detroit Electric car at the Historic White Pine Village in Ludington, just minutes from Cartier Mansion.

The carriage house where Kate Cartier parked her car.

1900s. While the suite pays homage to Cartier's history, it offers a modern ADA-compliant roll-in shower and accessible sink. The original woodwork accents the large windows.

You can stay in a private bedroom and bath in Kate Cartier's Blue Silk Room. Beautiful light-blue silken wall coverings adorn the walls, and the original crystal chandelier lights the room. The Blue Silk Room features a king-size bed, a private bath, and a claw-foot bathtub and shower.

CARTIER MANSION BED AND BREAKFAST

WHAT: A bed-and-breakfast that was once the home of Kate and Warren Cartier

WHERE: 409 E Ludington Ave., Ludington

COST: Varies depending on room rate and dates

PRO TIP: While most historic bed-and-breakfasts aren't ADA accessible, those with mobility challenges can enjoy the Cartier Mansion's beautifully renovated Carriage House, which features an ADA-accessible suite.

ROCK-SOLID BEAUTY

What are the pictures and sculptured land formations along Pictured Rocks National Lakeshore?

The National Park Service operates the Pictured Rocks National Lakeshore, the first of four national shorelines, where you'll find brilliant multicolored sandstone cliffs and waterfalls.

Groundwater emerging through cracks in the rocks and trickling down creates stunning-colored striations called pictures. Minerals paint the multicolored Pictured Rocks. The red and orange shades come from iron, the blue and green from copper, manganese produces blacks and browns, and the white comes from limonite.

Grand Portal, a beautiful arch, is the Pictured Rocks' highest point. Due to its size, 200 feet above Lake Superior, you can see it for miles. A boat gives you the best view of this rock formation.

Lover's Leap is also referred to as the Petit Portal Arch. A Native American legend tells of a Native American woman's loved one who never returned from a hunting trip. The legend says the heartbroken maiden threw herself off the cliff and died. Do not try jumping and swimming from Lover's Leap, as the waters below are shallow.

PICTURED ROCKS NATIONAL LAKESHORE

WHAT: A colorful shoreline with cliffs featuring named rock formations located on Lake Superior's south shore in Michigan's Upper Peninsula

WHERE: Between Munising and Grand Marais

COST: $20 admits the driver and passengers in a private vehicle for seven consecutive days. The fee does not cover camping, lighthouse tours, or other expenses.

PRO TIP: Pictured Rocks Cruise, a National Park Service concessionaire, departing from Munising, is the best way to see the Pictured Rocks National Lakeshore. The 32-mile round-trip boat ride is appropriate for all activity levels.

Battleship Row at Pictured Rocks National Lakeshore

In addition to Lover's Leap, other nature-made rock formations include Indian Head, Miners Castle, and Chapel Rock.

Spray Falls and Chapel Falls are the two Pictured Rocks National Lakeshore waterfalls. Chapel Falls is an 80-foot-high waterfall with water coming from Section Creek. In the 1940s, the archway connecting the rock to the mainland crumpled. Today, only tree roots join the two.

Lakeshore Trail goes to Spray Falls, the most remote waterfall. Spray Creek jets out over the Pictured Rocks cliffs, dropping into Lake Superior. The perfect spot to easily see Spray Falls is on the Pictured Rocks Cruises.

The 10-mile round-trip hiking trail at the Chapel Basin provides the best land view, where you can use a shuttle service to get to your starting point and then hike to your vehicle.

THE NEVER-ENDING JOB

What painting project is a continuous effort?

The Mackinac Bridge is a five-mile-long suspension bridge that spans the Straights of Mackinaw, connecting Michigan's Upper and Lower Peninsulas. Painting the Mighty Mac takes seven years typically; when they complete the job, it starts all over again. In the meantime, workers continually look for rusted areas and touch up those spots to prevent further damage.

The Mackinac Bridge Authority's in-house painting team uses a three-coat industry-standard process of exceptionally long-lasting paint, including a primer coat, intermediate coat, and urethane final coat. The distinctive green paint on the lower section of the Mackinac Bridge is a Foliage Green Federal Standard 595b, Color No. 14110. The white towers are Ivory Federal Standard 595b, Color No. 13711.

They use approximately 1,200 gallons of paint per year to complete the touch-ups. Repainting the complete Mighty Mac takes 135,783 gallons—7,280 gallons of ivory paint for the towers and 128,503 gallons of green for the rest of the bridge.

How was the green-and-ivory color scheme chosen in the first place? It turns out the selection process was relatively straightforward. Essentially, an ad agency picked the colors for the bridge. The agency worked for a company that supplied engines and equipment to build the bridge. They would feature an illustration of the bridge in the advertisement, but its colors hadn't been selected yet, so the ad agency used ivory and green in

---

Daily, the Mackinac Bridge only supports vehicular traffic. The exception is every Labor Day when the bridge closes to vehicles and thousands of pedestrians join the annual Mackinac Bridge Walk.

A view of the Mackinac Bridge from Colonial Michilimackinac showing the bridge's span

their image. The bridge authority liked the ad and picked the same color scheme for the actual bridge.

A more extensive painting project that began in 1999 and ended in 2017 was the first of its magnitude since they built the bridge. The bridge was stripped to bare metal and repainted entirely. The bridge needed an extensive repaint to remove the lead-based paint from the original paint job. The crew carefully removed the toxic paint, containing it during the process, and shipped it for appropriate disposal.

MACKINAC BRIDGE

WHAT: The fifth-longest suspension bridge in the world. When the bridge opened in November 1957, it was the longest in the world.

WHERE: Spans the lower and upper peninsula from Mackinaw City to St. Ignace

COST: Passenger vehicles are $4 per car. Others are $5 per axle.

PRO TIP: If you fear driving across bridges, use the bridge's free Drivers Assistance Program, available 24 hours a day, seven days a week. Call 906-643-7600.

AIN'T I A WOMAN?

Who was the first Black woman to sue a White man—and win?

Look at me, look at my arms, I have plowed, and planted, and gathered in the barns, and no man can head me. And ain't I a woman? I could work as much, and eat as much as a man when I could get it, and bear the lash as well. And ain't I a woman? I have borne 13 children and seen most all sold off to slavery. And when I cried out with my mother's grief none but Jesus heard me. And ain't I a woman?

—Sojourner Truth

In 1797, James and Elizabeth Baumfree welcomed a baby daughter and named her Isabella Baumfree. While her name included the word free, they were enslaved on the estate of Johannes. At nine, Isabella's master sold her without her parents to John Neely. He bought Isabella and a flock of sheep for $100. She stayed with the Neelys until 1808; then, John Neely sold her to Marinus Schryver, a tavern keeper in Port Ewen, New York, where she stayed for only 18 months. When she was 13, Schryver sold her to John Dumont, with whom she remained until age 29. It was from there that she escaped to freedom.

She eventually married an enslaved man named Thomas. Before her marriage, she had two children: James, who died in childhood, and Diana. Isabella had three children with Thomas: Peter, Elizabeth, and Sophia.

A tribute to Sojourner Truth

In 1799, New York passed a law to abolish slavery gradually. Later, a law from 1817 declared that all slaves born in New York before July 4, 1799, would be free on July 4, 1827. Dumont promised to emancipate Isabella before then but changed his mind in 1826. So, before the end of the year, Baumfree took her infant daughter Sophia and walked off, leaving behind the rest of her family.

She found assistance from Isaac and Maria Van Wagenen in New Paltz, who paid Dumont $20 for the cost of her labor until Emancipation Day. Then, she focused on finding her son, Peter, who had been illegally sold to a plantation owner in Alabama. The Van Wagenens helped her take the case to court. The court ruled in her favor, and Peter returned to New York in 1828. She was the first Black woman to win a lawsuit in court against a White man.

In her 40s, she renamed herself Sojourner Truth and began speaking publicly for equal rights nationwide. She fought for not only abolition but also women's suffrage. In the 1850s, Truth followed her daughters to Battle Creek, where she died in 1883.

SOJOURNER TRUTH

WHAT: Sojourner Truth Memorial

WHERE: At the corner of North Division St. and East Michigan Ave., Battle Creek

COST: Free

PRO TIP: From the memorial, walk down Michigan, turn left onto Capital Avenue, and on the corner of Capital Avenue is a rainbow-colored Sojourner Truth mural.

You can pay your respects to Sojourner Truth in Oak Hill Cemetery. Hedges frame her tall, white, tablet-shaped grave marker. You'll see her marker near the C. W. Post mausoleum.

AN ELEVATED EXPERIENCE

Where can you walk on the world's longest timber-towered suspension bridge?

SkyBridge Michigan, the world's longest timber-towered suspension bridge, spans McLouth and Disciples Ridge peaks in the heart of Boyne Mountain Resort. This 1,200-foot-long pedestrian bridge opened to foot traffic in the fall of 2022 and is often called Michigan's second bridge, second only to the Mighty Mac. Inspired by the Pure Michigan M in elongated form, the design took six months to complete.

Experiential Resources designed SkyBridge Michigan, grounding it in about one million pounds of concrete. SkyBridge Michigan's timber-frame design pays homage to northern Michigan's logging heritage. Two striking timber towers anchor the bridge. The towers stand approximately 52 feet high, almost 70 feet long, and weigh about 40,000 pounds each.

The experience begins with a chairlift ride to the mountaintop, followed by an open-air walk across a suspended five-foot-wide walking surface almost 118 feet above the valley floor. You can cross the bridge and then make a return trip for ample views

---

After a day on the wild side, enjoy Eagle's Nest, an indoor dining venue at the top of the Hemlock chairlift. For a casual meal option, the Disciples Overlook food truck sits on the far side of SkyBridge with outdoor firepits. On Saturday evenings, you can enjoy live music entertainment throughout the summer.

The SkyBridge at Boyne Mountain Resort in fall. Photo courtesy of Boyne Mountain Resort

and thrills. You'll find a 36-foot span of see-through glass flooring in the middle of the bridge for an unobstructed glimpse of the valley below.

Take your camera to capture the stunning panoramic view of Boyne Valley. The SkyBridge connects to Boyne Mountain's extensive paved resort trail system for extended daytime hiking. You can also capture some great images at night from the resort when the resort illuminates the bridge. Open year-round, every season offers a reason to take in the views of this architectural masterpiece.

SKYBRIDGE

WHAT: World's longest timber-towered suspension bridge

WHERE: 1 Boyne Mountain Rd., Boyne Falls

COST: Single visit: youth and adults, ages 11–69, $25; seniors 70+, $20; juniors, ages 3–10, $15; children under 2, free ($1 Go Card fee)

PRO TIP: Due to the suspension bridge dynamics, mobility equipment is not allowed on the SkyBridge. If you need a wheelchair, walker, or crutches, purchase a scenic lift ticket and view the SkyBridge from the SkyBridge Loop. Strollers aren't permitted, either.

BEYOND NUTS AND BOLTS

How did the world's largest lug nut end up in Lansing?

After announcing Lansing's minor league baseball team, the town awaited the team's name. The minor league already had the Midland RockHounds, the Great Lakes Loons, and the West Michigan Whitecaps. A lot rides with the association of a team name—mascots, logos, and cheers. The name was important to Lansing.

Finally, the day came when they announced Lansing's newly formed minor league team name. They would call the team . . . wait for it . . . the *Lansing Lugnuts*! According to the American Heritage Dictionary, a lug nut is "a heavy, rounded nut that fits over a bolt, used especially to attach an automotive vehicle's wheel to its axle."

WORLD'S LARGEST LUG NUT

WHAT: A giant lug nut on a smokestack

WHERE: 420 E Michigan Ave., Lansing

COST: Free

PRO TIP: You can park at parking meters on the street, parking ramps, or parking lots within a four-to-five-block area around the stadium.

To say the name was controversial is an understatement. The name, meant to honor Lansing's automotive heritage, was intensely disliked. The *Lansing State Journal* conducted a poll that indicated that 90 percent of the Lansingites "strongly disliked" the name. It was not a great start to the new team. With letters to the editor on both sides of the debate, the name gathered national attention from the *New York Times*, *USA Today*, *Sports Illustrated*, and *The Late Show with David Letterman*.

But the team wasn't giving up the name. They had successfully negotiated with the Hasbro toy company to relinquish the Lugnut trademark they had reserved for a future toy.

On the upside, the name led to a great cheer, "Let's Go Nuts!" And within 10 years, a *USA Today* poll in 2004 had America voting for the Lugnuts as the number one minor league team nickname.

Not long after the team started playing, an oversized lug nut was installed on top of a brick smokestack across the street from the ballpark. The silver lug nut weighs approximately 5,000 pounds.

Today, Jackson® Field™ is home to the Lansing Lugnuts, Lansing's minor league baseball team, a High-A Central League Eastern Division affiliate of the Oakland Athletics.

The world's largest lugnut

A PASSPORT TO CHANGE

What city is associated with the creation of the Peace Corps?

Senator John F. Kennedy reached the University of Michigan at 2 a.m. on October 14, 1960. He was ready to call it a day when he noticed a crowd of over 10,000 students waiting for him. With only three weeks before the election, he stepped to the microphone and delivered a three-minute unscripted speech in front of the Michigan Union. The address challenged the students to volunteer some of their lives to serve the nation by helping those in developing countries.

Kennedy questioned, "How many of you who are going to be doctors are willing to spend your days in Ghana? Technicians or engineers, how many of you are willing to work in the [US] Foreign Service? On your willingness . . . to contribute part of your life to this country, I think, will depend the answer whether a free society can compete. I think it can. And I think Americans are willing to contribute. But the effort must be far greater than we have ever made in the past." This early morning challenge is considered the Peace Corps founding moment.

JFK spent the night at the Michigan Union. The University of Michigan students, the university faculty, and the university's student newspaper, the *Michigan Daily*, obtained hundreds of signatures of students willing to serve worldwide. Six days before

---

While you're in Ann Arbor, visit the "Big House." The University of Michigan's football stadium is the largest in the United States and the Western Hemisphere. It is also the third-largest stadium in the world.

Left: *The Michigan Union where John F. Kennedy gave an unscripted speech about volunteer service.* Right: *A monument to where John F. Kennedy first proposed the Peace Corps. Photos by Alexis Dingman*

the election, Kennedy proposed "a Peace Corps of talented young men and women, willing and able to serve their country . . . as an alternative or as a supplement to peacetime selective service."

A few weeks after his inauguration, on March 1, 1961, Kennedy used an executive order to create the Peace Corps. The first director of the Peace Corps, Sargent Shriver, wrote in 1964, "It might still be just an idea but for the affirmative response of those Michigan students and faculty."

THE MICHIGAN UNION

WHAT: Historical marker at the venue where John F. Kennedy first defined the Peace Corps

WHERE: 525 S State St., Ann Arbor

COST: Free

PRO TIP: You'll find metered parking in front of the Union on both sides of State Street. Additionally, there's a visitor parking lot at 400 Thompson Street behind the Michigan Union.

BATTLING CHERRY PIE PANS

Where is the world's largest cherry pie pan?

A humongous slice of concrete cherry pie sits in a giant pie pan in Charlevoix, Michigan. Handmade wooden letters declare it the "World's Largest Cherry Pie." Approximately 50 miles away, in Traverse City, another sign boasts the "Guinness Book of World Records . . . Largest Cherry Pie" next to another giant pie pan. Both towns claim the record.

In 1976, during America's bicentennial celebration, Charlevoix, after building a pie pan and an oven big enough to hold it, successfully baked a 17,420-pound cherry pie during its annual cherry festival. They served approximately 7,000 people with about 10,000 slices of pie.

Then, in 1987, Traverse City's Chef Pierre Bakeries made a pie weighing 28,350 pounds and measuring 17 feet, six inches in diameter. The tin still stands on Cass Road in Traverse City. Jacklin Steel Supply Company built the pie pan for the record-setting pie. It was 18 feet wide and 26 inches deep. Bakery employees and hundreds of volunteers assembled, baked, and served the pie on baking day. People lined up and passed 510 buckets of cherry pie filling bucket-brigade-style into the pie pan. Finally, they added a top crust. At serving time, a tube served the filling from the pan's bottom into small cups.

WORLD'S LARGEST CHERRY PIE PAN

WHAT: Two pie pans, each claiming to be the world's largest

WHERE: 3424 Cass Rd., Traverse City, and 6591 US-3, Charlevoix

COST: Free

PRO TIP: You'll find a small parking lot on the side of the pie pan in Charlevoix.

Top: The Guiness Book of World Records *declared Traverse City's cherry pie the world's largest.* Inset: *World's largest cherry pie in Charlevoix.*

Then, they topped the filling with pastry crumbs. An estimated 35,000 spectators ate from the giant cherry pie.

The Guinness Book of World Records confirmed Traverse City's cherry pie as the largest ever, shattering Charlevoix's record. But the victory was controversial. Charlevoix argues that the Traverse City pie had no bottom crust, so it wasn't a complete cherry pie.

But within three years, the city of Oliver, British Columbia, shattered Traverse City's record. On July 14, 1990, they baked a 37,721-pound cherry pie. They officially broke the Traverse City record as the home of the "World's Largest Cherry Pie." But the Canadian pastry chefs forgot to save the pie pan, so Traverse City is still the leader in plus-sized pie pans.

Michigan grows 70 percent of the United States's supply of Montmorency tart cherries, making it the world's largest producer. Traverse City, known as the Cherry Capital of the World, hosts the annual National Cherry Festival.

CHILLAX WITH A BOOK

Why does one man use three different names?

It's not unusual for an actor or writer to adapt a new name for professional purposes. Norma Jeane Mortenson became Marilyn Monroe, while Samuel Langhorne Clemens became Mark Twain. While the name on the Chillermania author's birth certificate is Christopher Tod Wright, like many in the entertainment industry, he chose a stage name to begin his radio career. In 1983, he started his writing career at radio station WQON in Grayling. In 1987, he began his radio career at KHQ and chose the stage name Christopher Knight.

In 1998, after writing and producing thousands of commercials and voice-overs, he self-published an audiobook, *St. Helena*, under his stage name, Christopher Knight. Then, in 1999, the audiobook became a novel, followed by another novel in the same year, *Ferocity*. While writing *Ferocity*, he devised an idea for a kids' series that became the Michigan Chillers.

In March of 2000, Wright used the pen name Johnathan Rand to publish the first book in the Michigan Chillers series, *Mayhem on Mackinac Island*. Next came book two: *Terror Stalks Traverse City*. The books were an immediate success. Then, in 2001, he began the American Chillers series with *Michigan Mega-Monsters*, followed by the Freddie Fernortner Fearless First Grader series. Knight wrote additional adult novels. Then, more children's book series like Creepy Campfire Chillers, an audio group; three books in the Adventure Club series; the

If you have a budding young author, Johnathan Rand conducts two-hour classes, open to kids nine to 13, to show them how to create their own stories from beginning to end.

Inside Chillermania a bookstore selling only books by the author owner Johnathan Rand

CHILLERMANIA

WHAT: A unique author-owned bookstore where the author, Johnathan Rand, sells only his books.

WHERE: 1651 S Straits Hwy., Indian River

COST: Free to visit. Purchase prices vary.

PRO TIP: While Johnathan Rand is not always at the store, he frequents Chillermania with Brutus and Brody, his adopted shelter dogs.

Dollar $tore Danny series; and the Nightmare Nation series.

So, why did Christopher Tod Wright decide to write under two pen names? He continued to use the name Christopher Knight for his adult fiction. When he began authoring children's books, he wanted a separate brand for kids so parents knew they could count on age-appropriate material. He settled on the pseudonym Johnathan Rand.

Since publishing the Michigan Chillers in the spring of 2000, he's spoken at more than 2,200 schools and libraries throughout the United States and Canada. He takes an influential message with him on this journey. His mission is to let kids know if they can read, they can do anything. In 2005, he opened Chillermania in Indian River, where his audience can buy signed copies of his books and often meet the author, Johnathan Rand, in person.

In 2021, Christopher Tod Wright used his birth name to release an audiobook-only edition of *Meditative: Lessons in Practice, Persistence, and Perspective*, a semiautobiographical work that takes the listener on a journey to explore the wealth of creativity, imagination, and inner tranquility within their own mind. Combining all three of his names, he has nearly seven million copies in print of 120 titles.

WHEEL TURNED TIRE

What was the world's largest tire before it was a tire?

Driving down I-94 near the Southfield Freeway, you pass the world's largest tire and might think you'd find a giant tire because you're in the Motor City. The tire is 80 feet tall, weighs 12 tons, and can withstand hurricane-strength winds.

Initially, the humongous Uniroyal tire was a Ferris wheel designed for the 1964 New York World's Fair in Flushing Meadows–Corona Park in Flushing, Queens, New York. Owned by the US Rubber Company, a predecessor to Uniroyal, the 96-passenger Ferris wheel bore the name US Royal Tires after a brand of tires in the US Rubber Company portfolio. The Ferris wheel gave rides to more than two million people, including celebrities and dignitaries.

When the fair ended in 1965, they sent it to Detroit, where outside US Rubber's Midwest corporate headquarters, the Ferris wheel was reassembled as a tire without the gondola baskets. It was a stationary display. Since 1966,

THE UNIROYAL TIRE

WHAT: The world's largest tire

WHERE: I-94 near the Southfield Freeway, Allen Park

COST: Free

PRO TIP: The Uniroyal tire is on private property; however, you can easily see the tire from the expressway.

The Uniroyal tire as a Ferris wheel at the New York World's Fair in 1964.

the Uniroyal tire has been an icon of Metro Detroit, sitting on Interstate 94 in Allen Park.

The tire received several revisions throughout the years. Michelin bought the Uniroyal Goodrich Tire Company and refurbished the landmark. They modernized the tire, giving it a sleek new look, adding neon lighting to the Uniroyal lettering and a new hubcap. In 2003, they updated the neon lettering with reflective lettering and other interior work.

For more information about Detroit's automotive heritage, the Automotive Hall of Fame is about five miles away. Exhibits include early automobile history, the rise of the automotive industry worldwide, and automobile styling.

The Uniroyal tire as it stands today.
Photo courtesy of Alexis Dingman

REPTILIAN RETREAT

How did a family home grow into a sanctuary for alligators?

In the early 1990s, the Critchlows lived in the small town of Bellevue, where Mr. Critchlow had some tortoises. One day, a man approached him, asking if Critchlow would take care of his baby alligator while he was on vacation. The man instructed him on how to take care of the alligator and left town. The man never returned to pick up his alligator. The Critchlows now owned an alligator, and they needed to work it out.

Soon, word spread that the Critchlows would take it if you had an alligator you could no longer provide for. They continued to become home to more of the creatures until, over 15 years, they had 30 in the basement of their home—a standard house with a large backyard. Eventually, people wanted to see the alligators, so they charged a dollar for those who wanted to visit.

They realized they needed to do something different. In 2008, they purchased four and a half acres of land in the country, manually dug two ponds for the alligators, and began Critchlow Alligator Sanctuary. Their longest alligator is Godzilla, 11.5 feet long. They acquired him more than 25 years ago when he was five and a half feet long.

Each alligator has a story, a name, and frequently a troubled past. People purchase them as babies and don't want to keep them throughout their lives. Often, they come to the sanctuary after being found in drug raids. The animals may have been kept in closets, tanks, or bathtubs. After alligators have been raised

You can also purchase cups of alligator food specifically designed for their dietary needs to feed the alligators.

Rescued alligators living at the Critchlow Alligator Sanctuary

by humans, they can't go to the wild. So, they end up at Critchlow Alligator Sanctuary's unexpected location. One might expect to find an alligator sanctuary in Florida or New Orleans, but not in farming country near Battle Creek, Michigan.

Today, hundreds of reptiles have come to the sanctuary through donation, adoption, rescue, or from other institutions. The sanctuary works with state and local authorities, animal control organizations, and educational programs and internships through schools and universities. They don't buy, sell, or trade animals but provide a home and care for them for the rest of their lives.

CRITCHLOW ALLIGATOR SANCTUARY

WHAT: A reptile rescue facility that is open to the public

WHERE: 1698 M-66, Athens

COST: Regular admission, $12.95; seniors 60+, $11.95; service discount, $11.95; children 2 and under, free. Parking is free.

PRO TIP: Included in the price are guided tours of the sanctuary. Plan to spend one to two hours exploring.

TRASH TO TREASURE

When does the magic start to happen?

The American Museum of Magic's collection features about 3,000 advertising posters, and many have called it the Smithsonian for magic artifacts. The museum's walls, covered with posters advertising magic shows, tell an essential story of when the magic started. It all began long before the magician took the stage.

Magic shows evolved from street performances to full-blown stage acts. Along with that evolution came the transformation from simple posters with only text to stunning colored signs with pictured stories. Long before television and internet advertising, these posters advertised magic shows. The mystery and excitement drew people in. The advertisements would appear about two weeks before the show, telling the story of the fun to come, and after the show, they became trash. They'd be ripped down, thrown away, outdated and no longer relevant. Even if the show came to town again, an updated poster would appear rather than the original. Then, one day, people began collecting them, preserving history, illustrating the evolution of magic and its advertising. As you look around the American Museum of Magic, you will see examples of colorful and detailed posters and mass-produced advertisements, which connect to the evolution of advertising and magic shows.

AMERICAN MUSEUM OF MAGIC

WHAT: The most extensive collection of magic on public display in the Western Hemisphere

WHERE: 107 E Michigan Ave., Marshall

COST: Adults, $7; children, $4.50; children under 5, free. You'll find free parking on the street.

PRO TIP: The museum is in a historic 1860s building. You can only reach the second floor via a staircase.

A poster advertising Thurston with the devil imagery

Early examples were exclusively text with no images, just monochromatic black-and-white prints. From there, on the museum's walls, you can see an evolution of magic as a form of entertainment and magic in posters. Big words featuring the headline performers—Blackstone or Houdini. One massive word as a spectacle. Words like a marquee and the coming-soon feature presentation.

Magic shows evolved to include pretty women to attract those with other interests. The posters might say, "He's in the company of the 30 most gorgeous girls," to make the show more appealing to those who didn't care about magic. Some included animals that did a couple of tricks, and others used performers from the symphony. Magicians' acts evolved, so they came to make magic happen at every level.

Visitors can take a self-guided tour. The American Museum of Magic has two floors of original posters, props, and memorabilia from the 16th century to modern times. Visitors learn how magicians evolved from street performers to stage stars performing for royalty.

The oldest object in the museum is the first edition of *The Discoverie of Witchcraft* from 1584, the first printed English book explaining how to perform magic. A modern exhibit features magicians Penn & Teller's suits. If you want to get into the act yourself, squeeze into a replica of Harry Houdini's oversized milk can that he used for the Milk Can Escape trick.

On Saturdays at 1 p.m., the museum offers a complimentary magic show with your paid admission. You don't need a reservation for these family-friendly shows.

GIZZARDS GALORE

Where is the gizzard capital of the world?

Joe's Gizzard City has been in the Bristol family since 1960. The restaurant's ownership started with Ron and Ruby Bristol, who started the place as a diner. Ruby developed her famous batter mix and used it on chicken. The restaurant was a renowned chicken restaurant with the locals.

They've passed down the restaurant's ownership through the generations of the Bristol family, to Joe in the 1980s. Joe decided to put his spin on the place, and the restaurant transformed into Joe's Gizzard City, known for its world-famous deep-fried chicken gizzards made with the famous batter mix Ruby developed.

Chicken gizzards are the chicken's stomach. Because birds don't have teeth, they need a way to break down the food before it goes further into their digestive tract. As chickens peck, they gather bits of gravel and other debris. All that ends up in the gizzard, which uses a variety of enzymes and muscles to smash the food so that the chick can digest it. You'll often find a gizzard mixed with giblets when you buy a whole chicken or turkey.

Joe's gizzards are tender and not chewy because before deep-frying them, he cooks them in a pressure cooker. Then he batters and deep-fries them. While they're known for the gizzards, they have a complete menu featuring many batter-dipped fried proteins, like chicken, fish, and shrimp. You'll also find batter-dipped and

---

The town is so devoted to gizzards that they turned their local festival into Gizzard Fest. On the second weekend in June, more than 100,000 people descend on this small town of just over 3,000 to experience gizzard-eating contests, a beer tent, over 100 vendors, and carnival rides.

Left: *The entrance to Joe's Gizzard City in Potterville.* Top: *A basket of original gizzards at Joe's Gizzard City in Potterville.*

JOE'S GIZZARD CITY

WHAT: A restaurant specializing in chicken gizzards

WHERE: 120 W Main St., Potterville

COST: Varies depending on menu selection

PRO TIP: If you pay in cash, you will save four percent of the check.

fried vegetables, like mushrooms and cauliflower. If that isn't enough, all their desserts are deep-fried. You'll discover Twinkies, Oreos, cookie dough, elephant ears, and Joe nuts—all battered in Joe's famous batter mix and deep-fried. They also have salads for the faint of heart.

Joe's Gizzard City has been on Food Network's *Diners, Drive-Ins and Dives* twice. The host, Guy Fieri, developed their Triple D Burger—a third of a pound cheeseburger with pickles, onions, and a slice of tomato, dipped in Joe's famous batter mix and then deep-fried.

FIELD OF HONOR

Who plants a four-acre field of wildflowers and why?

Each year, Joan Donaldson and John Van Voorhees, co-owners and operators of Pleasant Hill Farm, combine a wildflower mixture that includes poppies, cornflower or bachelor's buttons, and daisies. Then, Van Voorhees plants four acres of the combination of flowers in the fall.

Sergeant Mateo Donaldson, their adopted son, served in Afghanistan, came home with post-traumatic stress disorder, and took his own life in February 2015. Before his service, he was Pleasant Hill Farm's beekeeper. Today, these flowers provide pollen for the bees and butterflies Matteo loved. They also assist in pollinating the farm's blueberries.

A sign requests, "Thank you for not walking on the flowers. They were planted to honor our son, Sgt. Mateo Donaldson (1981–2015) and Analilia Salinas (July 2000–July 2019)." Mateo's grave lies in Fennville Cemetery, about 70 yards from the poppy field. The field also honors a young family friend, Analilia Salinas, who died from bone cancer in July 2019.

The poppies bloom on Pleasant Hill Farm's field west of Fennville Cemetery. To view the field, park along M-89 and walk into the Fennville Cemetery. Alternatively, except on Sundays, you can park at the Assembly of God Church's parking lot.

SERGEANT DONALDSON AND ANALILIA SALINAS POPPY FIELDS

WHAT: Four acres of wildflowers, including an abundance of poppies

WHERE: 5897 124th Ave., Fennville

COST: Free

PRO TIP: Do *not* walk into the poppies but admire them from the edges of the field. Remember, the poppies are a tribute and should be respected.

Left: *A wildflower mixture that includes poppies, cornflower or bachelor's buttons, and daisies.* Right: *Sign explaining the purpose of the field. Photos by Alexis Dingman.*

The poppies bloom in southwest Michigan in June and are finished by the Fourth of July. Fewer flowers are in bloom later in the season.

In addition to Pleasant Hill Farm, Fennville features several opportunities for agritourism. Stop by Virtue Cider, Fenn Valley Winery, Salt of the Earth, or Crane's Pie Pantry and Apple Orchard while in the area.

WHAT YOU KNOW, YOU KNOW

Who started their acting career at the Ramsdell Theatre?

In 1969, James Earl Jones won his first Tony Award for *The Great White Hope*. Subsequently, he received his second Tony Award for portraying Troy Maxson in *Fences*. Then, in 1991, Jones received Emmy Awards for his roles in *Gabriel's Fire* and *Heat Wave*. But where did it all start?

James's father, actor Robert Earl Jones, left his family before he was born. James's grandparents raised him in Manistee. As a child, James had a stutter that became so severe that he didn't talk for eight years. As a form of self-expression, he began to write poetry.

The Ramsdell Theatre is where James Earl Jones started acting in high school during a production of *Othello*. Today, a painting of him during the show hangs in the theater. You'll also hear a 30-second audio greeting recorded by Jones at the beginning of every production at the Ramsdell Theatre, making it the only theater in America with an audio greeting by James Earl Jones.

Renowned Chicago architect Solon Spencer Beman designed the 100-year-old Ramsdell, now listed in the National Register of Historic Places. A local Manistee lawyer and philanthropist, Thomas Jefferson Ramsdell, built the theater and grand ballroom in 1903. Another fun fact about the theater is that Walter Wilcox Burridge,

---

Television and film actor Toni Trucks is another famous actor to get a start at the Ramsdell Theatre. Her credits include the hit CBS series *SEAL Team*. Other series regular credits include *Made in Jersey* and *NCIS: New Orleans*.

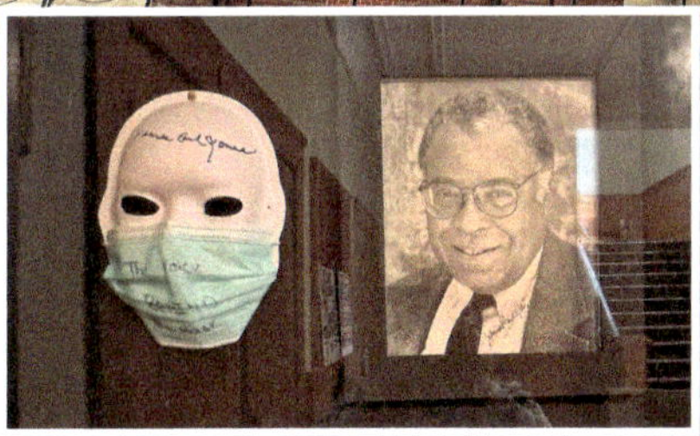

Top: *Historic Ramsdell Theatre on the National Register of Historic Places.* Inset: *The voice behind the mask—James Earl Jones*

a prominent painter who painted the original *Wizard of Oz* scenery, created the front drop curtain called A Grove Near Athens.

Today, the Ramsdell Theatre is a West Michigan center for arts—home to the Manistee Civic Players and the Manistee Art Institute. It hosts more than 200 events annually. In addition to musicals, plays and workshops, art exhibits, and classes, the Ramsdell is known for Metropolitan Opera live broadcasts and music concerts.

RAMSDELL THEATRE

WHAT: The theater where James Earl Jones began his acting career

WHERE: 101 Maple St., Manistee

COST: Varies depending on production

PRO TIP: The theater doesn't allow parking or drop-offs on Maple Street. You'll find free parking at First Street, the Methodist Church lot at 387 First Street, the public library lot at 95 Maple Street, and behind the Vogue Theatre on River Street.

FLOUTING THE DRY SPELL

How did this bar legally stay open during Prohibition?

The Two Way Inn sits at the corner of Nevada and Mount Elliott in Hamtramck, the oldest bar in Detroit. It's been there since 1876 when Colonel Philetus Norris founded the saloon. Over the last 150 years, the building has had many incarnations, from a saloon, a hotel, a dance hall, a stagecoach stop, a railroad station, a general store, and maybe even a brothel. In the basement, you'll find a jail cell to accommodate prisoners in transport. In the late 1800s, it could take weeks to transport criminals from one location to another by horse and buggy, so officials had intermediate stations en route.

The bar sports the original wooden floors from the 1870s, and the place on the floor that led to the basement's jail cell is also there. The owners removed the drop ceilings to expose the

TWO WAY INN

WHAT: The oldest bar in Detroit

WHERE: 17897 Mount Elliott St., Hamtramck

COST: Varies depending on menu selection

PRO TIP: They serve food on Wednesdays and Thursdays. Check out their Facebook page for what's on the menu.

Colonel Philetus Norris was also a surveyor, Civil War spy, cofounder of the National Park system, and poet. Rumor has it that Norris is another type of spirit you'll find at the Two Way Inn. Norris, often spotted in Western attire, is known as "the Cowboy" due to his wide-brimmed hat.

Top: *Exterior of the Two-Way Inn.* Inset: *Two-Way Inn sign. Photos courtesy of Alexis Dingman.*

original tin ceilings, but the original worn wooden booths and bar are still there. Each room features two ways for entering, said to be used for the chaser and the one chased, hence the name Two Way.

During Prohibition, upstairs was a dentist's office. In that era, doctors and dentists could legally prescribe alcohol for medicinal purposes. So, a quick trip upstairs to see the doc for that awful toothache and then return to the saloon with a prescription for a bit of spirit.

FLOUR POWER

What role did the windmill De Zwaan play in World War II?

A windmill called De Zwaan, Dutch for "the swan," ground grain into flour in the town of Vinkel, Noord Brabant, the Netherlands. During World War II, the windmill was a lookout, where people hid from the Germans at the top of the mill. Some survivors of the war believe that the windmill saved their lives.

In the 1950s, Holland's city officials sought a way to display their Dutch heritage. They settled on the iconic windmill. They went to the Netherlands, where government officials sold them De Zwaan. This wouldn't be possible today as the Netherlands has laws against exporting windmills. But in 1964, De Zwaan set sail for Holland, Michigan. The windmill was deconstructed and the pieces loaded onto a ship bound for America.

Once it arrived, workers modified the windmill to make it more efficient. In Holland, they replaced the large mound the windmill stood on with a three-story brick structure. Caught in combat in the Netherlands, bullet holes in the windmill's blades

THE DE ZWAAN WINDMILL

WHAT: The only working Dutch windmill in the United States

WHERE: 1 Lincoln Ave., Holland

COST: Adults, $12; children ages 3–15, $6; children under 3, free.

PRO TIP: Purchase some flour ground at the windmill, take it home, and bake some tasty treats.

De Zwaan is only one aspect of Windmill Island Gardens. They feature thousands of tulips in early May, during the Tulip Time Festival, and other beautiful gardens the rest of the summer.

Top: *De Zwaan windmill.* Inset: *Tulips during Holland's Tulip Time*

from that time tell an exciting story from World War II. You can easily see them in the base designed as a bench.

Today, the windmill turns between 12,000 and 15,000 pounds of grain into flour annually, and then they sell it to visitors at Windmill Island Gardens. You can take a self-guided windmill tour with docents available to ask questions. They also have a video tour for more in-depth explanations of the structure.

FROM AUTHOR'S HAVEN TO HISTORIC LANDMARK

Who brought hundreds of thousands of people closer to nature?

On the banks of the Shiawassee River, in Curwood Castle Park, stands James Oliver Curwood's writing studio, known as Curwood Castle. Curwood completed the replica of a Norman château in 1923, where it sits among other historic homes and buildings, and it is on the United States National Register of Historic Places.

It took Curwood, a native of Owosso, 10 years to sell his first story and then another 15 years to make a good living at writing. He was not an overnight best-selling author, but eventually, it came. Curwood published his novel *Kazan* in 1914, a story about a domesticated wolf-dog mix that traveled with his owner to the Canadian wilderness, told from the dog's perspective. He and his master become separated, and the animal ends up living with a wolf pack. The novel sold over 500,000 copies. Columbia Pictures made the novel into a movie in 1949.

A sculpture of James Oliver Curwood standing outside the castle

While in Owosso, you'll find three other small museums that tell more of the area's history: the Comstock Pioneer Cabin, the Woodard Paymaster Building, and the Amos Gould House.

Curwood Castle

CURWOOD CASTLE–WRITING & CONSERVATION STUDIO MUSEUM

WHAT: A small castle, now a museum, built by the author James Oliver Curwood

WHERE: 224 Curwood Castle Dr., Owosso

COST: Adults, $5; children under 10, $2

PRO TIP: Seasonally, open April 1 through December 31, 1 to 5 p.m., Tuesday through Sunday

In 1916, he authored a book based on his experience during a hunting trip in the Rocky Mountains and his encounter with a bear. In 1990, RCA Columbia Pictures released a motion picture entitled *The Bear* based on his book called *The Grizzly King*.

Curwood wrote about the immense Canadian wilderness. The Canadian government realized the popularity of his books and hired him to explore the prairie provinces and more remote northern regions. Collecting material for stories, he introduced settlers to Canada. Curwood is the only American the Canadian government ever hired as an exploratory and descriptive writer. Curwood brought millions of readers a closer appreciation of nature and wildlife through his writing.

RETRO RARITIES

Where can you take a plane ride into World War II history?

The Yankee Air Museum at the Willow Run Airport is affiliated with the Smithsonian Aerospace and Science Museum. They offer various interactive aviation experiences, and you can explore 20th-century exhibits from World War I to the Vietnam War. One unique activity at this museum takes a hands-on experience to a whole new level. You can book a trip on one of their five aircraft and journey through history. They offer in-flight rides in the B-25 *Rosie's Reply* bomber, the B-17 *Yankee Lady*, the C-47 *Hairless Joe Skytrain*, the UH-1 *Huey*, and the Ford *Tri-Motor*. The museum only offers flight experiences from May to October, so you must plan to cross this activity off your bucket list.

The Yankee Air Museum acquired the B-25D, known as *Rosie's Reply*, in 1987. This bomber battled in World War II and is one of only two B-25Ds still flying. Rosie's Reply is the same type of bomber that General Jimmy Doolittle and his raiders flew to deliver the first return strike to Japan on April 18, 1942. Everyone believed this daring mission would be a one-way flight as the 16 B-25s launched from the deck of the aircraft carrier USS *Hornet* had insufficient fuel to return or land at an air base in China. The Doolittle Raiders succeeded. Fifteen B-25s reached China but crash-landed. One landed in Russia. Seventy-seven of the eighty all-volunteer crew members survived.

The Yankee Warrior at the Yankee Air Museum.
Photo courtesy of Destination Ann Arbor

Top: Rosie's Reply. Bottom: The Yankee Lady. *Photos courtesy of Destination Ann Arbor*

THE YANKEE AIR MUSEUM

WHAT: An aviation museum at Willow Run Airport

WHERE: 47884 D St., Belleville

COST: Adults, $13; seniors (60+), $10; veterans and military, $10; Children ages 2–17, $10; children under 2, free

PRO TIP: Most of the plane ride cost is a charitable donation.

The B-25 is the only American military aircraft named after a person, General Billy Mitchell. He is often referred to as the "godfather of military aviation." Manufacturers built *Rosie's Reply* (B-25D serial no. 43-3634) on December 8, 1943, then delivered the plane on December 17, 1943, to the US Army Air Forces. This aircraft flew in the 12th Air Force, 340th Bombardment Group, in the 489th Bomb Squadron. It is known to have flown eight combat missions out of Corsica.

If you're not up for a ride in the historic aircraft, explore the *Deep Landings* exhibit, where you can pilot in one of their flight simulators.

RESPECT AND REMEMBER

How did this man survive the atomic bomb on Nagasaki?

During World War II, Master Sergeant Kenneth Rice was one of the 987 survivors of the Bataan Death March. His captors put him on a Japanese hell ship, a term used by the Allied POWs that referred to vessels commandeered by the Japanese Empire to transport POWs. Then, they used the boat to force laborers to locations under Japanese control. An American submarine sunk the ship. Since Rice was on the upper deck, he survived, while those below deck were less fortunate. When they found him, he was clinging to a barrel in the middle of the ocean. He said he would still hold onto that barrel even if he drowned.

The Japanese took him to Japan to work in the labor camps alongside Dutch prisoners. He chose to work in the mines at the labor camp, while some worked at the docks. One day, suddenly, something shut off the air vents to the mine. It wasn't clear what was happening. They went three days without air. Finally, Rice and his buddy said they must figure out what was happening. So, one of

MICHIGAN HEROES MUSEUM

WHAT: The museum shares the personal stories of heroism, leadership, and sacrifice of everyday Michigan men and women thrust into extraordinary circumstances.

WHERE: 1250 Weiss St., Frankenmuth

COST: Adults, $7; seniors and veterans, $6; students (ages 18 and under), $3; children 5 and under, free. Parking is free.

PRO TIP: Among the stories is the world's largest, publicly displayed collection of Medals of Honor. You'll find 30 Medal of Honor recipients exhibited in a dedicated gallery. They include each recipient's medals and other personal items.

Left: *The Michigan Heroes Museum.* Right: *Military Equipment outside the Michigan Heroes Museum*

them went topside to investigate, and he returned and said, "You guys will not believe this. There aren't any Japanese guards up there. There's nothing but sunrise."

The prisoners, who had been working in the mine, were a mile and a half underground when the atomic bomb was dropped on Nagasaki. Ken Rice survived the nuclear bomb and did a tour of duty in the Korean War. He survived the Korean War. Finally, he went on to work with the Saginaw County Sheriff's office until he retired.

This story is only one of the almost 1,000 displays housed in the Michigan Heroes Museum, each containing the stories and personal items belonging to Michigan men and women who answered their nation's call to service.

LUGE YOUR MIND

Ever wondered what it's like to "luge" life in the fast lane?

Luge was a traditional 16th-century Swiss sport. It became a Winter Olympic sport in 1964. To luge, an individual lies face up, feetfirst on the luge sled, and speeds down the luge track. A luger uses their calf muscles to flex the runners or applies pressure from opposing shoulders to the seat to steer. The fastest luger across the finish line wins.

The Muskegon Luge Adventure Sports Park, inside the Muskegon State Park, is one of only four luge tracks in the United States. Three-time Olympian Frank Masley designed the 850-foot track, which includes two starting areas and six curves. Even though this track is shorter than the Olympic luge tracks in Salt Lake City and Lake Placid, you'll find it's the perfect length for first-time luge athletes. Before speeding down the only artificial track made from

MUSKEGON LUGE ADVENTURE SPORTS PARK

WHAT: One of four luge tracks in the United States

WHERE: 462 Scenic Dr., North Muskegon

COST: Varies depending on the activities package: summer wheel luge, $20; winter luge rates vary.

PRO TIP: You'll need a Michigan DNR Recreation Passport to park at Muskegon Luge Adventure Sports Park. You can purchase one at the park if you don't already have one.

Muskegon State Park is open year-round. They offer various sporting activities, including ice, skating, cross-country skiing, snowshoeing, and winter zip-lining. In addition, they feature archery, zip-lining, and trail quests in the summer.

Top: *Wheel luge designed for summer use.* Inset: *Winter luge. Photos courtesy of Adam Alexander Photo*

natural ice that isn't refrigerated, you'll receive training and the proper equipment. Be aware you can reach speeds of up to 30 miles per hour. While luge is typically a winter sport, the Muskegon Luge Adventure Sports Park offers a wheeled version for summer fun.

The activities at Michigan Luge are universally accessible through special equipment and adaptations. The sports park will also discuss ways to adapt various activities to fit your individual needs.

TIMELESS VIGILANCE

Where is the world's oldest continuously operating fire station?

October 1871 was a great fire period in the Midwest. Chicago, Holland, Manistee, and several other towns suffered catastrophic losses during this time. The total burned property loss in Manistee alone was about a million dollars. In today's dollars, that's over 23 million.

By the late 1880s, a major agenda item at the Manistee city commission meetings was a requirement of a proper municipal structure for the fire department. Finally, the city hired Saginaw architect F. W. Hollister to draw up specifications for the new building. Hollister had also been the architect of Manistee's principal school. By October 1888, they advertised a request for proposal. The lowest bid came from the local firm of Gore A. Brownrigg & T.N. Reynolds, for $7, 516.

On June 17, 2019, the Guinness World Records designated the historic Manistee Fire Station at 281 First Street as the "Oldest Continuously Manned Operating Fire Station." Firefighters have fully staffed the station 24 hours a day, seven days a week, 365 days a year as a paid professional fire department since it opened on June 17, 1889.

MANISTEE FIRE HALL

WHAT: The world's oldest continuously operating fire station

WHERE: 281 1st St., Manistee

COST: Free

PRO TIP: Tours of the Manistee Fire Station are available if the crew isn't out on calls or during mealtimes if the group is smaller than six. For larger groups, the fire station suggests calling for a reservation.

Manistee Fire Hall

The firm completed the two-story, pressed-brick, and cut-stone building in the spring of 1889. The building featured French plate glass and trimmed galvanized iron. Firefighters moved in without much attention. The unique cross-gabled Romanesque Revival–style building features a two-and-a-half-story copper-domed tower and hasn't changed its design or usage since it was built.

The firehouse also features a small display of artifacts and photos on the history of Manistee's Fire Department.

REMEMBER THE RAISIN!

Where did the battle cry "Remember the Raisin" originate?

In August 1812, Americans surrendered Detroit to the British-Native Alliance. So, on January 18, 1813, the goal of the first Battle of the River Raisin was to regain Detroit. As they were waiting for the army to gather, River Raisin settlers begged Brigadier General James Winchester to take back their settlement from the British and Native armed occupation. The general, his Kentucky militia, and the American settlers took on the British and Natives in an attack that resulted in the British and Natives retreating across the frozen river. The Americans liberated the River Raisin settlement.

The second battle, on January 22, 1813, was one of the largest during the War of 1812. Native forces, British soldiers, and Canadian militia conducted a surprise counterattack. They forced General Winchester to surrender. The result was Tecumseh's American Indian Confederation's most significant victory and the worst defeat for the United States. Of the 1,000 Americans who fought, only 33 escaped capture or death. Fifteen percent of the American army was lost.

The River Raisin had several names throughout history. The river's floodplains formed an extensive sturgeon breeding ground that led into Lake Erie. So, Native Americans called the river "Nummasepee" or "River of Sturgeon." With abundant wild grapes growing along its banks, French explorers referred to it as "La Rivière aux Raisins," translated as "The River with Grapes." The British simply called it the River Raisin.

Left: *The Visitor Center at the River Raisin National Battlefield.* Right: *A diarama of the River Raisin National Battlefield.*

RIVER RAISIN NATIONAL BATTLEFIELD PARK

WHAT: An interpretation of the January 1813 Battles of the War of 1812

WHERE: 333 N Dixie Hwy., Monroe

COST: Free

PRO TIP: Open daily from 9 a.m. to 5 p.m. except Thanksgiving, Christmas, and New Year's Day. The battlefield grounds are open from sunrise to sunset.

The cry didn't come from the Battles of the River Raisin, but instead the day after the two battles. On January 23, 1813, the wounded Americans, primarily Kentuckians, remained in the Frenchtown homes. Native allies of the British conducted a surprise attack on those Americans and killed most of the 60 to 65 remaining. During that attack, they cried, "Remember the Raisin!" The rallying cry "Remember the Raisin" garnered support during the rest of the war.

The visitor center exhibits include dioramas and full-size soldiers from all three forces. Take time to view the 17-minute film on the Battles of the River Raisin.

FROM COCOA TO CURDS

What is chocolate cheese?

Frankenmuth Cheese Haus started making their cheese in-house to guarantee quality. They make seven savory cheese spreads in-house and two sweet flavors: blueberry and strawberry. They use all fresh ingredients, like onions rather than onion powder. One of their most unusual cheeses is chocolate cheese, of which they offer three varieties: chocolate peanut butter, chocolate mint, and regular chocolate. They describe chocolate cheese as a cross between Tootsie Roll® and fudge, a creamy cheese, while not a spread. The initial recipe came from Michigan State University. Chocolate cheese begins with a Monterey Jack cheese base, to which they add cocoa powder and powdered sugar. After they mix that all together in a large stand mixer, they put it into a metal frame mold. They refrigerate the product overnight and then cut it into blocks of chocolate cheese. You can even watch them make the cheese.

William "Tiny" Zehnder, known as Mr. Frankenmuth, opened the Cheese Haus on May 28, 1968. It became a second-generation business when Judy Zehnder Keller took over the company from her father in 1980 and operated it for 42 years. Today, Judy's daughter, Martha Zehnder Kaczynski, leads the business.

The building is an impressive homage to Bavarian architecture, with a 2,000-pound, 23-feet-tall copper onion dome on top

CHEESE HAUS

WHAT: A third-generation, family-owned business carrying more than 270 different types of cheeses from around the world

WHERE: 545 S Main St., Frankenmuth

COST: Varies depending on selection

PRO TIP: Have your picture taken with the store's mascot, Claus the Cheese Haus Mouse.

Left: *A display with three kinds of chocolate cheese.* Right: *Claus the Cheese Haus mouse.*

of the Figurinespiel Tower. A mural on the side of the building represents the days of traditional Bavarian cattle drives, along with members of Judy Zehnder Keller's family.

Today, the Cheese Haus carries more than 270 international and domestic cheese types, many made in Michigan. In addition to cheese, you'll find other Michigan-made products, such as Michigan-made wine.

You can explore their sausages, jerkies, old-fashioned candy, preserves, and honey. They also have a gourmet kitchen section, so you can stock up on everything you need to create a perfect charcuterie board.

The 74-foot Figurinespiel Tower at the Frankenmuth Cheese Haus describes an animated story about cheese-making across Europe and the United States. "The World of Cheese" story plays at 9 a.m., 11 a.m., 2 p.m., 5 p.m., and 8 p.m. daily.

LYRICAL LANDMARK

Who wrote one of the world's most popular hymns?

"So, I'll cherish the old rugged cross,
till my trophies at last I lay down;
I will cling to the old rugged cross,
and exchange it some day for a crown."

—George Bennard

The Bennard family welcomed an infant son named George on February 4, 1873, in Youngstown, Ohio. His father, a coal miner in Iowa, passed when George was 16. After his father died, he worked in the mines for a short time to help support the family. Eventually, he worked with the Salvation Army and became a traveling minister, holding revivals throughout the Midwest.

Inspired by young hecklers, Bennard looked to scripture and reflected on Christ and the cross. He began to see them as inseparable. In 1913, Reverend Bennard wrote the well-loved hymn "The Old Rugged Cross." First came the song's melody, and then he wrote the first verse in Albion over several meetings. He completed the final three verses in Pokagon, where Reverend Bennard led meetings at a local church.

Near Reverend and Mrs. George Bennard's home, north of Reed City, history buffs erected a memorial cross on September 14, 1954. Later, the Old Rugged Cross Historical Museum became an extension of that memorial. Today, those artifacts have become the Reed City Heritage Museum.

Left: *Reverand Bennard's guitar sits on top of his wife's piano.* Right: *Reverand George Bennard author of the Old Rugged Cross.*

The song moved them to tears when he performed the final hymn to Reverend Leroy Bostwick and his wife, Ruby. First, he sang accompanied by a guitar and then with an organ, violin, and choir. You'll find a historic marker in Albion where he wrote the song.

During his lifetime, George Bennard wrote the words and music to over 300 songs, the most famous being "The Old Rugged Cross."

REED CITY HERITAGE MUSEUM (FORMERLY THE OLD RUGGED CROSS HISTORICAL MUSEUM)

WHAT: The museum features exhibits containing mementos and relics about George Bennard and Reed City.

WHERE: 138 W Slosson Ave., Reed City

COST: Free. Donations encouraged.

PRO TIP: Bennard wrote the hymn at his home at 1101 East Michigan Avenue in Albion; however, the museum telling the story of his life and creation of the hymn is in Reed City. In Albion, only a historical marker exists.

MECHANICAL MARVELS

What enchanting secrets lie within Marvin's Marvelous Mechanical Museum?

Marvin's Marvelous Mechanical Museum sits at the crossroads of museum and arcade—a whimsical wonderland that beckons you to discover its secrets. The museum's allure begins with its facade, an amalgamation of nostalgia and modernity, luring you in with a display of vintage signs, quirky sculptures, and mesmerizing kinetic art. As the doors swing open, a captivating symphony of sights and sounds greets visitors, setting the stage for an immersive journey into the unknown. The flashing lights and sounds can put you into sensory overload.

Mysterious gadgets come to life within this eclectic domain, each with a story to tell. The curious will find themselves drawn to a mechanical fortune teller, a mystical automaton that dispenses cryptic prophecies with an air of mysterious wisdom. Nearby, a mesmerizing Rube Goldberg machine sends marbles on an intricate, unpredictable journey, eliciting awe and amazement at the complexity of its design.

Amid the array of restored antique coin-operated games, whispers of the past echo through the air, transporting you to eras long gone. The museum's founder, Marvin himself, has gathered these vintage gems, preserving the nostalgia of simpler times and sharing it with a new generation.

MARVIN'S MARVELOUS MECHANICAL MUSEUM

WHAT: Five thousand square feet of vintage coin-operated machines; morbid, unusual nostalgia; weird things; and the newest video game crazes

WHERE: 31005 Orchard Lake Rd., Farmington Hills

COST: Free admission. Machines run on quarters and range from 25 cents to $1.

PRO TIP: Marvin's has a café that offers free Wi-Fi.

Top: *The welcome sign at Marvin's Marvelous Mechanical Museum.*
Inset: *A vintage arcade machine.*

One of the most captivating spectacles is the collection of vintage arcade games, each evoking fond memories of carefree days as a youth spent in arcades. Generations intertwine as young and old compete, laughing and cheering amid the nostalgic ambiance.

The banks call Marvin's Marvelous Mechanical Museum when they're short on dollar bills, five-dollar bills, and quarters and ask them to make a deposit.

THE OTHERSIDE UNVEILED

Is it paranormal or haunted?

Haunted dolls for sale online command significant prices to accompany their mind-blowing experiences. But caveat emptor. Buyer beware. Not all dolls sold as haunted fit the criteria. So, before you buy, it pays to understand the difference between paranormal dolls and haunted dolls. A guided tour at the Otherside Paranormal & Mortuary Science Museum will assist in understanding the difference.

Haunted items have three main characteristics. First, they provide intelligent responses as opposed to random answers. Second, they have a high electromagnetic field (EMF) reading, and finally, they are intelligent spirit boxes. Paranormal items that have no intelligent responses may have a high EMF reading but are not a spirit or entity of any type.

The museum features an entire exhibit of dolls, from haunted to paranormal dolls. The type that nightmares are made of. Sarabina, the resident haunted doll at the museum, carries a lot of energy and connection to many who meet her. Before visiting the museum, she worked as a prop in several dark art studios and haunted houses. She'll remain at the museum as their in-house

---

Also in REO Town Marketplace is Voodoo's World of Oddtiques. This shop offers relics, taxidermy, skulls, medical specimens, collectibles, metaphysical items, books, and one-of-a-kind and handcrafted items. While you can purchase items from this shop, many are reminiscent of things you would find in a museum.

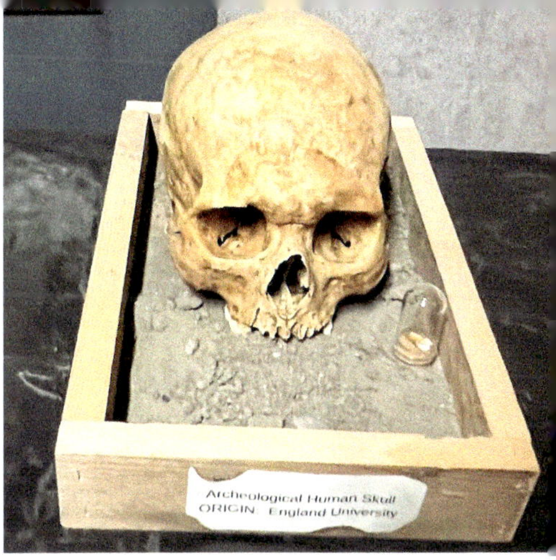

Left: *Paranormal and haunted dolls.* Right: *An archaelogical human skull.*

THE OTHERSIDE PARANORMAL & MORTUARY SCIENCE MUSEUM

WHAT: A guided-tour museum exploring the paranormal and mortuary science

WHERE: Inside REO Town Marketplace at 1023 S Washington Ave., Lansing

COST: Free. Donations accepted.

PRO TIP: Located inside the REO Town Marketplace, the museum's hours are Thursday through Sunday, noon to 5 p.m.

ghost girl, where many around her feel increased anxiety and stress.

The museum also has the Azazel doll, which was relocated from Georgia. Investigators found her as part of a paranormal investigation of an elderly woman's home. The woman's troubling activity stopped when they removed the doll from the house. Troubling but not haunted.

Included in the same space, you find displays of mortuary science. You'll learn about embalming from collections of early 20th-century embalming machines. View a human skull, an embalming table, and caskets.

NO CARS ALLOWED

What is the only state highway that doesn't allow motorized vehicles, and why?

Mackinac Island sits in Lake Huron, between Michigan's Upper and Lower Peninsulas, in the Straits of Mackinac. In 1898, officials banned cars and other motor vehicles on the island after a motorcar backfired and startled a horse. That ban remains today, except for a few emergency vehicles generally kept out of sight.

According to the Michigan Department of Transportation, M-185 is "the only state highway in the nation where motor vehicles are banned." The 8.004-mile-long state trunkline highway circles Mackinac. Michigan built the highway in the early 20th century, and they designated it a state highway in 1933. In 1960, they paved the highway, and in 1980, they needed to rebuild parts of the highway due to shoreline erosion.

They call the highway Main Street in the downtown area and Lake Shore Road throughout the rest of the island. The only traffic on the highway is by bicycle, horse, horse-drawn carriage, or on foot. Electric bikes are also typically banned, except for Class I, which they permit for those with mobility challenges. M-185 passes by several attractions on Mackinac Island,

MACKINAC ISLAND

WHAT: M-185 circles Mackinac Island, yet the island doesn't allow motorized vehicles.

WHERE: Located in Lake Huron, between Michigan's Upper and Lower Peninsulas

COST: No entrance fee to the island; however, the cost to ride the ferry round trip on Shepler's Ferry is adults, $34; children ages 5 to 12, $23; children 5 and under, free.

PRO TIP: Shepler's Ferry departs Mackinaw City in the Lower Peninsula and St. Ignace in the Upper Peninsula. Prices in either city are the same.

including Mackinac Island State Park, Fort Mackinac, British Landing, Arch Rock, and Devil's Kitchen.

Until an accident in 2005, it was the only state highway without any motor vehicle accidents. The only known accident happened when the island's fire truck damaged the door of their ambulance. The vehicles were responding to a report of an injured passenger on a ferry requiring medical attention.

While you're on the island burning off all those calories—hiking, biking, and riding horses—take time to sample some of the island's world-famous fudge. You'll find fudge shops from seven different companies offering free samples.

A team of horses pulling a carriage on Mackinac Island

GHOSTLY FOOTPRINTS

Are those ghost footprints on the bar?

You'll find artisan brews and unexplained phenomena woven into an air of mystery around the historic 120-year-old Mitten Brewing Company building, the Engine House No. 9. Owners Chris Andrus and Max Trierweiler embarked on their journey in February 2012, ready to breathe new life into the old engine house. Intrigued by the building's storied past, they couldn't resist asking a former tenant about potential hauntings. Half-jokingly, they received an unsettling response: "Just know that it's nothing bad." That remark planted a seed of curiosity.

One night during the second week of operation, Chris Andrus, the last person to leave the Engine House, returned early the following morning to find something bizarre in the lobby. Inexplicable footprints decorated the floor. As Chris pondered their origin, he realized they were a child's footprints. Leading to nowhere, they appeared as if from nothing.

Perplexed, Chris knew no one else had been in the building between his departure and return. Stranger still was the arrangement of the prints; they began and ended in the middle of

---

While housed in a former fire station, the brewery features a baseball theme, starting in the lobby with four blue stadium-style seats from the original Detroit Tiger Stadium. An old English D symbolizing the Detroit Tigers adorns the exposed brick wall with historic black-and-white baseball images. Ashwood, used to make baseball bats, continues the theme on the restaurant's tabletops.

Left: *Mitten Brewing Company exterior view.* Right: *The draft selection at Mitten Brewing Company.*

the room, pointed in all directions, with no discernible path. No one had entered, and no one had left. "I was the last one out and the first one in. There's really no practical explanation to the footprints," Chris said, reflecting on the eerie experience.

As time passed, more peculiar incidents unfolded. In April 2014, as Max Trierweiler and a manager performed upstairs demolition, they made another astonishing discovery. A visible white footprint lay inside a wall, shielded from the light of day for 126 years. Remembering the story and photo of Chris's experience, they compared the prints, and to their amazement, they matched.

The significance of this compelled the owners to preserve it. Carefully removed from the wall, they placed the footprint at the center of the upstairs bar top, sealed under an epoxy, and made visible for patrons to see, further showcasing its possible permanent tenant.

The question remains: who, or what, is this presence? The possibilities are endless, from a former firefighter who perished in Engine House No. 9's line of duty to the spirit of a child playing amid the wooden beams. While the truth may forever elude us, the Mitten Brewing Company's haunted past adds an irresistible charm to this establishment.

THE MITTEN BREWING COMPANY

WHAT: The white footprinted board is now part of the upper-level bar.

WHERE: 527 Leonard St. NW, Grand Rapids

COST: Free admission. Price varies depending on menu selections.

PRO TIP: Order a pizza flight along with your beer flight.

ALL ABOARD

What makes this train depot the most photographed rail station in the United States?

The Durand Union Station, nestled in Durand, stands out against the surrounding flat farmland. It appears massive for a small-town depot, but in its prime, circa 1912, 42 passenger trains, 78 freight trains, and 22 mail trains passed through the station every 24 hours. Some say it bears the honor of being the most photographed rail station in the United States. This historic gem, built in 1903, captures the imagination of photographers and travelers alike with its stunning architectural details.

DURAND UNION STATION

WHAT: Reputed to be the most photographed rail station in the United States

WHERE: 200 S Railroad St., Durand

COST: Free. Donations to the museum are encouraged.

PRO TIP: In addition to the active Amtrak passenger station, visit the area of the building that is now a museum.

Now on the National Register of Historic Places and the Michigan Register of Historic Places, the exterior of the building, initially built in the Chateau Romanesque style, exhibits a simplified Romanesque architectural style due to a fire in 1905. The 239-foot-long building features a facade of Missouri granite brick and Bedford cut stone. While it originally had a slate roof, they covered the roof in red clay tile after the fire. The upper level features dormers, and the towers with conical roofs lend a castle-like appearance to the building.

Stepping inside transports you to days gone by. One of the most striking features of the Durand Union Station's interior is its meticulously restored terrazzo tile flooring. As you walk

Left: *Exterior view of the Michigan Railroad Museum.* Right: *A display entitled "A Day in the Life of a Depot Agent."*

across the tiles, you can't help but feel a connection to the past, as if they are retracing the steps of generations of travelers before you.

In addition to its architectural splendor, the Durand train station holds historical significance. Serving as a vital transportation hub during the heyday of the railway era, it witnessed the ebb and flow of countless passengers. It played a crucial role in connecting communities and fostering economic growth. Today, the Durand station is an Amtrak center for rail travel, serving as a link from Port Austin to Chicago. However, the station stands as a living testament to the rich history of rail travel and architectural elegance, attracting photographers and history enthusiasts alike, eager to capture and preserve the timeless beauty of this remarkable piece of American history.

The Michigan Railroad History Museum occupies half of the Durand Union Station. In addition to exhibits specific to Durand's railroad history, the displays also feature general information on railroad history.

FROM SKELETONS TO SPIRITS

Where can you get your picture taken holding a human skull?

In the heart of Mt. Clemens sits an attraction that piques the curiosity of those seeking to explore the mysterious realm of mortality—the Anatomy of Death Museum. Unlike any other museum, this establishment delves into the intricacies of death, shedding light on the scientific, cultural, and historical aspects of this inevitable part of life.

Todd La Rosa, owner and curator, founded the Anatomy of Death Museum when he recognized the need to demystify the finality of death and educate the public about death and dying practices from around the world. This offbeat museum opened in 2019 and has garnered attention from locals and tourists, drawing a diverse crowd. It's been said this museum will "creep out the creepers." With more than 55 human skulls, skeletons, caskets, coffins, and embalming tables, among other death-related items, it holds the title of Michigan's Creepiest Attraction. You can even hold a human skull to have your picture taken.

Upon entering the museum's unassuming facade, you're transported into an immersive experience that covers a wide range of topics related to death. They begin by revealing death's mysteries behind a curtain of body bags. The Anatomy of Death is a captivating and educational testament to the human fascination

---

Inside the same building, you'll find Michigan's largest oddities and curiosities shop, where you can purchase various unusual items. You can buy things like glass skulls and funerary art.

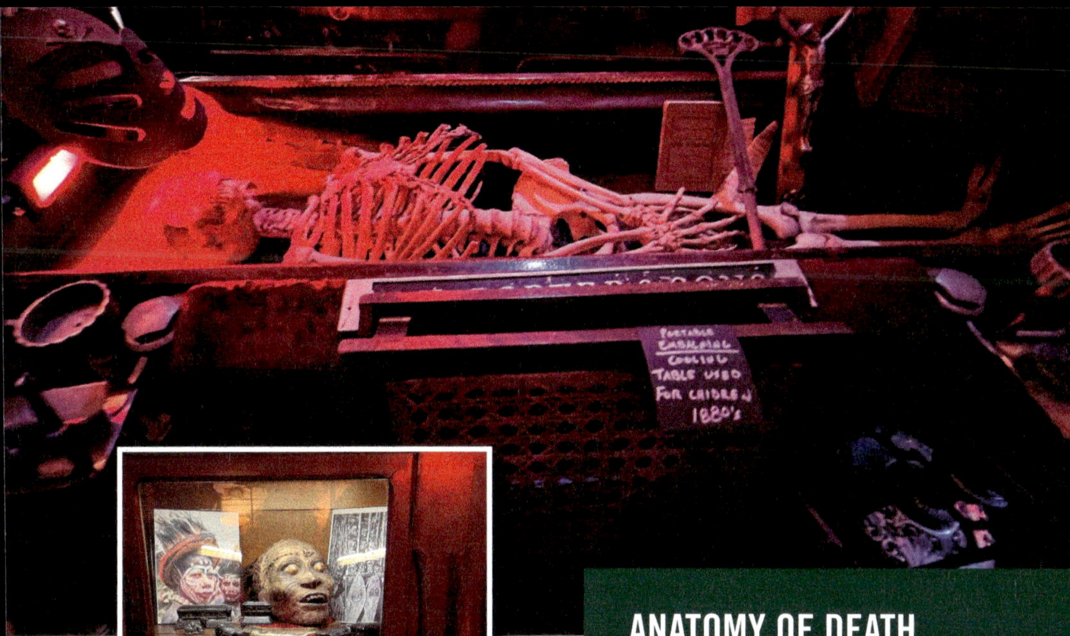

Top: *A portable embalming cooling table used for children in the 1880s.* Inset: *An early 20th century Septik tribal ancestor modeled over a real human skull.*

ANATOMY OF DEATH MUSEUM

WHAT: Michigan's only death museum

WHERE: 292 Cass Ave., Mount Clemens

COST: Adults, $10; children 14 and under, $7; children 5 and under, free

PRO TIP: The material in this museum can be sensitive. You'll want to be in the right frame of mind to enjoy this educational experience.

with mortality. It not only unravels the mysteries surrounding death but also encourages visitors to contemplate the significance of life itself. The museum serves as a reminder that death is a natural part of our existence.

One exhibit illustrates the Sepik tribal traditions from Papua New Guinea of over-modeling a human skull so that after adding clay to the skull, it would have a face that resembled the deceased. They would add shells, beads, and often the actual hair of the deceased, and then they would place the skull in a sacred area to watch over and protect the living.

UNLOCKING THE MYSTERY

How does this mechanical marvel raise and lower vessels to accommodate the elevation difference between the two Great Lakes?

Sault Saint Marie, affectionately referred to as the Soo, lies at the intersection of Lake Superior and Lake Huron, about 50 miles north of the Mackinac Bridge. One of the main attractions is the Soo Locks, an engineering marvel. While they have an observation tower to watch the boats locking through, you can also pass through them on a boat tour. In addition to experiencing passage through the locks, the tour provides a narrative history.

These impressive waterway marvels have played a pivotal role in shaping the history of the Great Lakes region, facilitating maritime trade, and connecting the heart of North America to the rest of the world.

When the Poe Lock finished in 1896, it marked a turning point. With its impressive 1,200-foot length and 100-foot width, the Poe Lock revolutionized the transportation of products like iron ore, coal, and grain. Its construction dramatically increased the capacity and efficiency of the Soo Locks, making it the world's largest lock at the time.

SOO LOCKS BOAT TOURS

WHAT: Ride on a boat and experience passing through the locks.

WHERE: Dock location: 1157 E Portage Ave., Sault Saint Marie

COST: Adults, $30; children ages 5–16, $10; children 5 and under, free. Observing boats pass through the Soo Locks from the observation tower is free.

PRO TIP: To find out when freighters will pass through the locks, check their schedule at 906-253-9290.

A view of the Soo Locks from a boat as they are opening

Today, the Soo Locks consist of four locks—the MacArthur Lock, the Poe Lock, the Davis Lock, and the now-closed Sabin Lock. The MacArthur Lock, the smallest of the four United States locks, was completed in 1943 and measures 800 feet in length. The Davis Lock, built in 1914, is 1,350 feet long, while the Sabin Lock, constructed in 1919, measures 1,200 feet. However, the Poe Lock remains the primary workhorse with its impressive size and capacity. A fifth lock sits on the Canadian side strictly for pleasure boats.

The Poe Lock's operation utilizes a gravity-fed system, relying on the natural elevation difference between Lake Superior and Lake Huron. Massive gates at either end of the lock open and close, allowing ships to enter, and then water is released or filled to raise or lower vessels to the appropriate level. This process enables ships to navigate the 21-foot drop between the two lakes.

The Poe Lock requires an astonishing 22 million gallons of water to position a boat.

SEEING THINGS

Why is there a giant pink elephant in front of a pizzeria?

Rest assured, it isn't an alcohol-induced hallucination. It isn't you! Pink elephants do exist, at least on the east side of Michigan. With its curled trunk reaching as high as the pizzeria's rooftop, the enormous pink elephant is a landmark to identify a one-story, relatively obscure building. The elephant makes giving directions easy: "You can't miss it. Just look for the giant pink elephant in front."

Although it has traveled around town a bit, the pink elephant is a Mio icon, traveling around town since sometime in the 1970s. It once stood in front of a pink party store and gas station near the M33 trailhead at Bull Gap. That store has been gone for years, but the elephant moved to a restaurant across the street from the pizzeria. The previous owners of Mio Pizza Shop bought the pink elephant from a restaurant across the street in approximately 2008. No one is exactly sure of this giant's age.

While the story of how the giant pink elephant came to one of Michigan's tastiest pizzerias is a bit vague, it certainly is a draw. People come from around Michigan to have their picture taken

---

A giant red elephant is also a landmark outside Nowicki's Sausage Shoppe at 107 South Third Street in Rogers City. Nowicki's has been making sausage since 1917 and has several locations throughout Eastern Michigan. Only the Rogers City store has the elephant.

with this fun pachyderm. On a warm day, sit outside at one of their picnic tables and enjoy your pizza in front of the landmark. In addition to pizza, you'll find Dots, bite-sized crazy sticks topped with butter, garlic, and Parmesan cheese. Try one of their fresh salads or warm sandwiches if you're not in the mood for pizza.

GIANT PINK ELEPHANT

WHAT: A giant pink elephant acting as a landmark in front of Mio Pizza Shop

WHERE: 421 S Morenci Ave., Mio

COST: Free to see the pink elephant. Menu selection prices vary.

PRO TIP: Order your pizza first, then take your picture with the elephant while waiting for your order. Please don't climb on the elephant.

A giant pink elephant in front of Mio's Pizza Shop in Mio

LISTEN TO THE TREES

What happened when a man bought 200 acres of farmland but realized the land's condition made it more suited to horticulture use?

In 1926, when Harry Fee, a businessman from Adrian, retired, he purchased 200 acres of land surrounding Hidden Lake. He intended to start farming the ground, but given the conditions, he realized horticulture would be more rewarding than agriculture. Fee created landscape scenes on the land using flowers, brush, and trees.

In 1945, he donated his land to Michigan State University to "preserve and enhance the natural beauty of the gardens and to display plants for the inspiration and education of the public." Hidden Lake Gardens has 755 acres to explore indoor and outdoor spaces. The indoor plant conservatory features exotic plants and tropical settings. Outdoors, you can trek five miles of hiking trails. You can also see one of the most extensive bonsai collections in the Midwest.

Bonsai Tree

The Hidden Lake Gardens bonsai collection started in 1968 when they hired bonsai expert Jack Wikle.

An attraction added in 2023 is the ADA-accessible Canopy Walk, 65 feet above the ground and spanning 700 feet, where you can wander through the treetops. The walk allows you to observe nature in the treetops up close. You can explore wildlife, like insects and birds, up close through the trees' leaves and branches.

Arid Biome at the Conservatory in Hidden Lake Gardens

Open from late April to early November, the Hidden Lake Garden Bonsai Courtyard displays their bonsai collection outside the conservatory. Typically, they have 20 bonsai on display at any time, with more than 80 trees in their collection.

The variety of miniature trees in pots invites you to see the interaction between the hand-designed natural world and artistic imagination. Gifts from numerous accomplished bonsai artists grow in the garden with constant care. The bonsai collection showcases the crossroads of science and art.

HIDDEN LAKE GARDENS

WHAT: 755 acres of gardens, an arboretum, trails, and a canopy walk

WHERE: 6214 Monroe Rd. (M-50), Tipton

COST: Adults ages 18–64, $10; seniors 65+, $8; youth ages 11–17, $12; active military and veterans with ID, $8; students K–12 and college with ID, $5; children 4 and under, free

PRO TIP: The staff of Hidden Lake Gardens encourages you to interact with their team on Thursdays as they give special attention to the bonsai trees to train and maintain them. The Canopy Walk is a half-mile walk from the visitors center. Please call 517-431-2060 in advance to request reasonable accommodations.

SMALL WONDERS

Where can you find several homes inside a house?

While there's a fascination with the world's largest anything, which explains all those oversized roadside attractions throughout the United States, just as impressive is the other end of the spectrum, where miniatures amaze. Francis Light dreamed that one day she would have a space for people to experience miniatures as fine art. In 2007, the dream became a reality when the National Miniatures Trust established the Midwest Miniatures Museum inside a farmhouse on the Gilmore Car Museum's property in Hickory Corners. As time evolved, eventually, the museum moved to the Robbins House in Grand Haven.

The Midwest Miniatures Museum displays reproductions in four scales—the largest is the 1:12 scale, while the smallest is the 1:144 scale. Their permanent collection includes scale-model buildings representing various architectural styles and lifestyles. They have lifelike miniature dolls and fine-art dollhouses.

They feature vignettes of individual scenes or miniature rooms called room boxes. At the

MIDWEST MINIATURES MUSEUM

WHAT: Fine-quality miniatures exhibited in a historic mansion

WHERE: 20 S 5th St., Grand Haven

COST: Adults, $8; children ages 6–17, $5; children under 5, free

PRO TIP: You'll find 14 parking spots for cars available, with drop-off parking for buses. Buses have available parking nearby.

Explore the Education tab on the Midwest Miniatures Museum website for project templates you can print and complete at home.

same time, they have historical reproductions like a mid-century modern multi-story home, an auto garage, and a grocery store—a favorite is a model of Vincent van Gogh's famous yellow house.

You'll also find collections of unique miniature art pieces, including water crystal pieces and fine silver collections. More than 200 kachina dolls add to the fun.

The Midwest Miniatures Museum in Grand Haven, Michigan

GALACTIC GETAWAYS

How does the historic Keweenaw Mountain Lodge harness the power of darkness to elevate the guest experience?

In 1934, the Keweenaw Peninsula had the dubious distinction of having the nation's highest unemployment rate, at just over 72 percent. The country was in the middle of the Great Depression, and President Franklin D. Roosevelt established the Works Progress Administration to get the country back on its feet. Those workers built the Keweenaw Mountain Lodge. The lodge has been on the National Register of Historic Places since 1980.

While historically, the lodge preserved jobs, it's preserving the dark sky today. Nestled amid the Keweenaw Peninsula's landscape, Keweenaw Mountain Lodge has taken a giant leap toward protecting the natural wonders of the night sky by becoming an internationally designated dark sky park. This initiative has transformed the lodge into a hub of celestial exploration and a haven for stargazing enthusiasts.

With light pollution encroaching upon many parts of the world, dark sky parks have emerged as sanctuaries of natural darkness, allowing visitors to experience the unadulterated night sky. Keweenaw Mountain Lodge's designation as an international dark sky park represents a commitment to safeguarding the beauty of the night.

Taking great images of the dark sky is more than a shot in the dark. Participate in one of their night-sky photo workshops to learn to capture them intentionally. Keweenaw Mountain Lodge staff lead these sessions throughout the year. Check their events calendar.

A comfortable gathering space in the lobby of the Keweenaw Mountain Lodge

KEWEENAW MOUNTAIN LODGE DARK SKY PARK

WHAT: Historic resort and internationally designated dark sky park

WHERE: 14252 US Hwy. 41, Copper Harbor

COST: Free to visit the dark sky park. Overnight accommodation prices vary.

PRO TIP: Stays at the Keweenaw Mountain Lodge have a minimum two-night requirement.

As the sun sets behind the mountains and darkness envelops the landscape, Keweenaw Mountain Lodge comes alive with celestial wonders. Here, away from the glare of urban lights, a dramatic array of stars, planets, and galaxies come into view. Imagine stepping out of your cozy cabin, looking up, and being greeted by aurora borealis. Guests of the lodge and the public can participate in various activities celebrating the night sky.

The dark sky park status also opens up new opportunities for astrophotography enthusiasts, who can capture awe-inspiring shots of distant galaxies and the Milky Way stretching across the horizon. You'll leave with a newfound appreciation for the fragility of our planet's precious dark spaces and a determination to protect them.

PRETTY AS A PICTURE

How did a water conditioning plant come to have art that rivals any museum?

You might expect a building that serves as a water conditioning plant to be solely functional and essential but not beautiful. In the 1930s, Franklin Roosevelt's New Deal and the associated Works Progress Administration (WPA) initiatives got Americans back to work. In April 1938, those workers began construction on the Lansing Board of Water and Light's John F. Dye Water Conditioning Plant. This WPA project provided approximately 300 jobs, keeping workers busy for about a year. During that time, the federal government also hired more than 10,000 artists to create art throughout the United States as part of the same program. The artwork took many forms: murals, fine arts, theater, music, and writing. The John Dye Water Conditioning Plant features five examples of this New Deal art: three murals and two sculptures, one of which functions as a fountain.

Surrounded by children representing Lansing, Aquarius—the mythical Greek water carrier—graces the building's exterior. Samuel Cashwan created *Aquarius*, a limestone relief, between 1938 and 1939.

Inside the front door, a blue ceramic sculpture by Clivia Calder depicts two girls grooming themselves. The statue also

---

About 1987, a worker noticed the murals had suffered the test of time and needed repair. Frank Cassara, then 75 years old, agreed to restore the murals he painted and the Charles Pollock mural. He created the murals in his early 20s, then returned 50 years later to restore them. The project lasted an entire summer.

Charles Pollock's 1941 mural Water as Hydro-Electric Power depicts man's power over water.

CASSARA AND POLLOCK MURALS

WHAT: Three murals in the main lobby of the Lansing Board of Water and Light's John Dye Water Conditioning Plant

WHERE: 148 S Cedar St., Lansing

COST: Free

PRO TIP: To see the murals, you must make an appointment by using the contact form located at the bottom of the home page at lbwl.com. However, the exterior limestone relief is readily visible.

functions as a fountain featuring a water theme. Around the sculpture, two stairways ascend to a lobby flanked on three sides by hand-painted murals.

Frank Cassara created the murals on each side in 1940. *Water as Destructive Element* tells the story of flooding while *Beneficial Force of Water* illustrates water for cleaning and recreation.

On the back wall, Charles Pollock's 1941 mural *Water as Hydro-Electric Power* depicts man's power over water—hydroelectric power, agriculture, and industry. Jackson Pollock, the abstract expressionist, is Charles's younger brother.

VINTAGE VIEWS AND VINO

What careers prepared the founders of Chateau Chantal to be the perfect hosts?

In 1983, Robert and Nadine Begin founded Begin Orchards, which eventually became Chateau Chantal Winery and Inn in the Old Mission Peninsula outside of Traverse City. Originally a cherry farm, the 65-acre estate includes 40 acres of planted grapevine and features classic European-style wines. They farm a total of 100 acres and source additional grapes from Argentina.

The story of Chateau's founding couple, Robert and Nadine, is intriguing. Their previous careers were in service: Robert as a Catholic diocesan priest and Nadine following a similar path with the Felician Sisters. Eventually, both sought a different life, and Robert started over as a businessman with a construction company. After teaching home economics for 22 years, Nadine also began again.

Robert and Nadine married in 1974 and followed Robert's dream to build a European-style winery château. Their first careers of service to others gave them the skills to become the perfect hosts. The name Chantal means endearing, and their goal is to make the winery endearing through their hospitality. Today, the Begins' daughter and the winery's namesake, Marie-Chantal, leads the winery.

CHATEAU CHANTAL

WHAT: A vineyard, winery, and bed-and-breakfast

WHERE: 15900 Rue de Vin, Traverse City, Old Mission Peninsula

COST: Varies depending on experiences and purchases

PRO TIP: Make reservations early for the Thursday evening Jazz at Sunset events.

President and CEO Marie-Chantal Dalese at the Chateau Chantal tasting room

In addition to traditional wine tastings, Chateau Chantal offers cooking classes from January through May. You'll learn to create dishes that perfectly complement the winery's portfolio. They offer Jazz at Sunset, where you'll spend an evening listening to live jazz while enjoying a glass of wine overlooking the stunning vistas of Grand Traverse Bay.

To experience more Old Mission Peninsula and the Traverse City area, Chateau Chantel offers a bed-and-breakfast-style lodging with stunning views of the vineyard.

URBAN OASIS

Where can you find an enchanting island getaway right in the middle of the city?

Tucked away on an island in the Detroit River, minutes from downtown Detroit, the 985-acre Belle Isle Park is an urban oasis. It's just over the MacArthur Bridge, approximately three miles from the Renaissance Center. While you can return to nature here with the Belle Isle Nature Center, kayaking, lakes, canoeing, and fishing opportunities, you can also find urban attractions, like an aquarium, conservatory, and museum.

Belle Isle Aquarium is the oldest aquarium in the United States. It still features the original arched ceiling with stunning green tile, giving the aquarium an underwater feel. With more than 100 fish species, including those from the Great Lakes and throughout the world, you'll want to spend at least an hour here.

The Anna Scripps Whitcomb Conservatory covers 13 acres, including a lily pond and formal garden. The conservatory features five distinct areas: the Tropical House, a sunken fernery, the Palm House, the Cactus House, and the Show House. Flowering plant exhibits rotate in the Show House. On a typical day, you won't need to walk far to enjoy the conservatory or aquarium. You

Belle Isle Aquarium in Belle Isle State Park

The Livingstone Memorial Lighthouse, located at the island's north end, is the oldest in the United States built from marble. Unfortunately, they don't offer public tours even though it's a working lighthouse.

can park right in front. You'll also find a complimentary track chair if you have mobility challenges.

Belle Isle Nature Center offers an array of nature activities for tots to adults. You'll find activities like clouds and mud for the littles, while adults will have fun on their nature walks. While there isn't a charge for their programs, you must go to their website and register, as they have limited space for each program.

Dossin Great Lakes Museum explains Detroit's role in the area's maritime history. In addition to the indoor exhibits, they have various outdoor artifacts, including the anchor from the *Edmund Fitzgerald*.

BELLE ISLE PARK

WHAT: A 985-acre island park located in the Detroit River near downtown Detroit

WHERE: 99 Pleasure Dr., Detroit

COST: A Recreation Passport is required for the park; residents pay $13 annually; nonresidents pay $11 for a day pass, $39 annually. Admissions to museums, the aquarium, and the conservatory are free.

PRO TIP: While there aren't any restaurants on the island, you can purchase food from food trucks throughout the park during the peak season.

Anna Scripps Whitcomb Conservatory in Belle Isle State Park

UPCYCLING AT ITS BEST

Why did John Makinen build his house from bottles?

Born in Finland in 1871, John J. Makinen moved to Kaleva in 1903. He owned and operated a local pop bottling plant, Northwestern Bottling Works. After building a warehouse for pop, he noticed that it didn't freeze during the winter. So, he concluded that glass was a good insulator.

Like most people during the Great Depression, he didn't waste anything. Makinen built his house in 1941, using 60,000 glass bottles rejected due to flaws or chips. He used a variety of clear and colored pop bottles arranged horizontally, bottoms out, and connected with mortar. He placed the bottles using his creative and artistic side, making exciting designs for the house's exterior. You'll find diamond patterns and the words Happy Home spelled out, proudly proclaiming its design.

KALEVA'S HISTORICAL BOTTLE HOUSE MUSEUM

WHAT: A house and museum made mostly of bottles

WHERE: 14551 Wuoksi Ave., Kaleva

COST: Free

PRO TIP: Open Saturday and Sunday, Memorial Day through Christmas, noon to 4 p.m.

The Makinen Tackle Collection is an unusual museum collection purchased from Wisconsin collector Bill Gregory. He had amassed an example of every piece of fishing tackle made at Kaleva's Makinen Tackle Company during the 1950s and 1960s.

Top: *The Kaleva Bottle House from the exterior.* Inset: *Close up of the Kaleva Bottle House and the designed made from bottles.*

Makinen finished his home the same year he turned 70; however, he passed away before he could move in. Today, the Kaleva Bottle House is a historical museum with showrooms displaying artifacts from the Kaleva area. The museum's exhibits include those telling the story of Finnish American history. It's listed on the National Register of Historic Places and in Ripley's Believe It or Not!

THE ROARING RIVER

Where do waterfalls and wilderness create a symphony for the senses?

Just west of the small town of Paradise, near the center of Michigan's Upper Peninsula, sits Tahquamenon Falls State Park, Michigan's second-largest state park. The 46,179-acre state park offers more than 35 miles of trails to take maximum advantage of viewing the Upper and Lower Tahquamenon Falls.

At 200 feet across and a drop of 50 feet, the Upper Falls are the largest waterfalls in Michigan, one of the largest waterfalls east of the Mississippi River. You'll hear the roar in spring, with 50,000 gallons of water thundering over the falls every second. Tahquamenon Falls is second in volume only to Niagara Falls.

The Lower Falls, located four miles downstream, is a series of five lesser falls that cascade around

TAHQUAMENON FALLS STATE PARK

WHAT: A state park with two waterfalls

WHERE: 41382 W M-123, Paradise

COST: A Recreation Passport is required for the park; residents pay $13 annually; nonresidents pay $11 for a day pass, $39 annually.

PRO TIP: Don't rely on your GPS; have a map, as cell service is unreliable.

The Upper Tahquamenon Falls is busiest between 1 and 4 in the afternoon. You'll find multiple accessible views of the falls without taking stairs. To get even closer to the falls, use the optional 94-step staircase.

The Upper Tahquamenon Falls. Photo courtesy of UPTravel

an island. One of the best ways to view the Lower Falls is by renting a rowboat from the park concession, picking up those paddles, and rowing over to the island.

Tannins leaching from nearby cedar trees cause the river's amber color. Finally, the soft water agitated by the falls' movement results in the river's trademark foam. The combination of color and foam will please your sense of sight. You'll appreciate why locals nicknamed it "Root Beer" Falls.

YES, CAPTAIN!

What unique challenges did South Haven's first lighthouse keeper face?

Located at the Black River's mouth, the South Haven South Pierhead Light sits at the south pier's west end. The lighthouse, lit in 1872, still operates today. The existing tower replaced the original 1872 wooden building, and the original catwalk connects the light to the shore. Built in 1903, the South Haven Light has a black lantern on top of a red cylindrical tower. They mounted a Fifth-Order Fresnel lens made in Paris. In 1913, the tower's original location was no longer acceptable, and they moved the cast-iron lighthouse 425 feet to the end of the pier.

South Haven's first lighthouse keeper, Captain James S. Donahue, was appointed in 1874 after service in the Civil War, where he was wounded and lost a leg at the hip. Captain Donahue famously lit and extinguished the lighthouse faithfully every single day, making the trek in all seasons on one leg. South Haven legend states that folks maintaining the building have heard footsteps—a single footstep walking through the home, doors opening by themselves, and other phenomena. During his 35-year tenure as South Haven's lighthouse keeper, Donahue is credited with saving more than a dozen lives from the teeth of Lake Michigan.

They built the lighthouse keeper's home, a two-and-a-half-story, hipped-roof house made from wood in 1872. They

SOUTH HAVEN SOUTH PIERHEAD LIGHT

WHAT: A lighthouse purported to be haunted

WHERE: Water St., South Haven

COST: Free

PRO TIP: While the tower isn't open to the public, you can walk on the pier and take pictures from the beaches.

South Haven Lighthouse Waves. Photo courtesy of Drake Olmstead and the South Haven Visitors Bureau.

moved the home to 91 Michigan Avenue, and today, it serves as the Michigan Maritime Museum's Great Lakes Research Library.

After enjoying a day at the beach, stop by Clementine's in downtown South Haven for a bite. Once a bank, the building features a menu with Michigan ingredients like yellow lake perch and cherries.

ILLUSIONS AND ENCHANTMENT

Why is this town the Magic Capital of the World?

Born Harry Boutin, we all know the magician by his stage name, Harry Blackstone. Harry Blackstone and his brother Pete looked a lot alike. Although they weren't twins, their similar appearance wasn't bad in the illusion business.

They were on the road as the great Frederick until World War I came along. "Frederick" was offered a job for six weeks then but had to change his name. They said it was too much of a Germanic-sounding name. Walking down an Ohio street, he looked up and saw Blackstone Cigars. He said his car wheels were Blackstone and decided that would be his name.

Blackstone and his wife came to Michigan near Kalamazoo to escape the Chicago heat. In the early 1920s, theaters typically closed during the summer because theaters didn't have air-conditioning in those days. His wife went out for the day and came across the little village of Colon. She started looking around and found about 200 acres for sale, including a barn, a house, and some little cottages. Colon was the perfect location as it was halfway between the large cities of Chicago and Detroit, where he often performed. At his wife's urging, Blackstone visited Colon and decided to move there. He lived there during the summers from 1926 until the early 1950s, when he left the stage.

Harry Blackstone was the first magician to pull a rabbit from a hat. He performed that trick about 80,000 times during his career.

Left: *The gravesite of the Gwynnes, the Royal Family of Magic.* Right: *Harry Blackstone's gravesite*

While most magicians can fit their props into a small suitcase, Blackstone required two freight cars to carry his equipment. He employed many assistants, including a handsome young man and many petite girls that could squeeze into a box—necessary for the illusion business.

The magic business boosted Colon's local economy.

LAKESIDE CEMETERY

WHAT: A cemetery where many famous magicians are buried, including Harry Blackstone

WHERE: North Farrand Rd. near the intersection of Colon Rd., Colon

COST: Free

PRO TIP: The graves of magicians are easily identified from Memorial Day through the beginning of October with playing cards fixed on a magician's wand. You'll find many of the magicians' graves on the cemetery's south side.

A BRIGHT IDEA

Where can you see one of the world's largest light bulbs?

The Grand Trunk Railway constructed the building in 1858, to aid in carrying freight and people from Port Huron to Detroit and back. This railway linked Port Huron to the rest of the world. Housed in the historic Fort Gratiot train depot, the Thomas Edison Depot Museum is where Thomas Edison worked as a news reporter from 1859 to 1863. Edison sold fruits, vegetables, candy, and newspapers on the journey between the cities.

Thomas Edison referred to his time in Port Huron in his writings and conversations. The museum tells the story of the Edison family's move between Ohio and Port Huron. As a young boy, Tom was curious, and his mother fostered this, encouraging his science studies. He worked on trains in the historic depot. He repeatedly experienced setbacks in his inventions until Edison, the inventor, finally created the light bulb. You can learn about his contributions to society in the museum's theater and interactive displays.

On display, you'll find the 50,000-watt light bulb, part of a mock-up of a proposed memorial to Thomas Edison that admirers never built. In 1940, the giant light bulb stood atop the temporary monument used at the movie premiere of the MGM biographical film *Young Tom Edison* starring Mickey Rooney. Edison's wife lit the bulb at the movie premiere.

THOMAS EDISON DEPOT MUSEUM

WHAT: A museum dedicated to Thomas Edison's life and work

WHERE: 510 Thomas Edison Pkwy., Port Huron

COST: Free

PRO TIP: The Thomas Edison Depot is fully wheelchair accessible.

Top left: *An exhibit at the Thomas Edison Depot Museum in Port Huron.* Above left: *A sculpture of the young Thomas Alva Edison in front of the Blue Water Bridge.* Right: *One of the world's largest lightbulbs.*

The exhibits portray Edison's story of creativity, family support, adversity, perseverance, and ultimate triumph as one of the greatest inventors of our time. You can apply your imagination as you learn about Edison's inventions.

The St. Clair Tunnel, the world's first international tunnel, linked Port Huron with Canada. It was an international submarine railway tunnel built in 1891, 2,290 feet underwater and 11,725 feet long.

A SECRET PASSAGE

Why did a United States Post Office have a secret passage?

Officials dedicated the Castle Museum as a post office on July 3, 1898. The building's architect, William Martin Aiken, claimed he chose French Renaissance Revival architecture inspired by the early French settlement of the Saginaw Valley. The building's architectural style is an unusual choice for a post office.

The building quickly became a valued local landmark. As the City of Saginaw grew, the building grew to meet the city's expanded requirements. By the mid-1930s, the building had become insufficient for the community's needs, and the federal government proposed the construction of a new facility on the site. This proposal met community-wide opposition, and plans were created to enlarge the existing building. The 1937 addition kept the original building design. It preserved the Federal Avenue facade.

When the building was originally constructed as a post office in 1898, there were no surveillance systems or security cameras like we have today. Besides letters, people were mailing valuables like gold jewelry and cash to family members and friends. The postal system needed a way to protect the things that people were mailing, so they built observation galleries from catwalks around their mail sorting rooms. The postmaster general would patrol those rooms through little peepholes, where he would observe everybody in the sorting room to ensure they weren't opening people's mail and taking things or reading things that they shouldn't. The postmaster had his own entrance to the building;

The Saginaw County Sports Hall of Fame, located within the Castle Museum, celebrates the legacies of sports figures within the Saginaw County region.

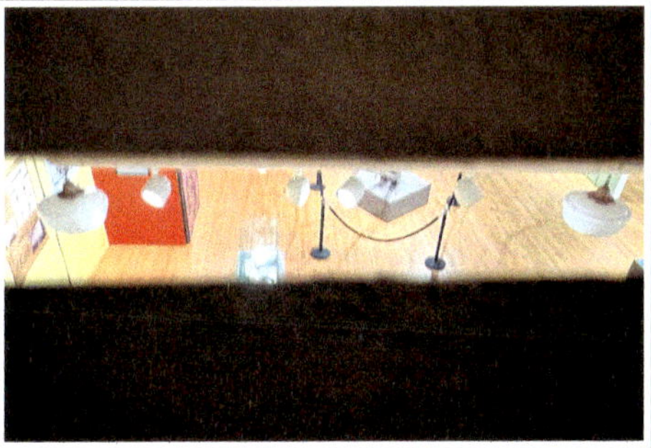

Top: *The Castle Museum in Saginaw.*
Inset: *A peep hole from the observation gallery where the postmaster watched the mailroom employees.*

THE CASTLE MUSEUM

WHAT: A museum in a former post office that was designed as a castle

WHERE: 500 Federal Ave., Saginaw

COST: Free to Saginaw County residents; non-Saginaw County residents: per person, $3; family, $5; senior citizens 65+, $2

PRO TIP: You'll find a free parking lot behind the museum with an accessible ramp.

so employees never knew when they were under observation. They always needed to be acting appropriately.

The rooms on the observation deck were black, so nobody could tell when somebody was observing them. Even if the little flap was open, it remained dark. If postal employees were caught misbehaving, they were punished by losing their jobs and livelihood.

FROM EIGHT TO GREAT

Why build a barn with eight sides?

A prominent Gagetown banker, James Luther Purdy, traveled through Iowa and came upon an octagon-shaped barn. He decided that he would build a similar structure near his hometown. He purchased 40 acres in 1895 and eventually bought a total of 560 acres, which includes where the buildings stand today.

The government encouraged octagon-shaped barns because the shape was a more efficient use of wood. The circular shape offers a larger volume-to-surface ratio than traditional rectangular or square barns, resulting in round barns using less wood, a limited resource. Additionally, storms rolled around the round barn, making the octagon barn less likely to be destroyed in a storm than a traditionally shaped barn.

The problem was that they needed a mathematician from the school to do 22½° angle-cuts. It was challenging to make the change from the square 90° angle. So, they didn't construct many round barns.

In 1991, the State of Michigan Department of Natural Resources (DNR) bought 80 acres of the 560 from the bank for $49,500. The DNR wanted the land because it linked two parcels already part of the Gagetown State Game Area. But, the DNR didn't want the buildings, which had fallen into disrepair. Their solution was to sell the structures or have them demolished.

THUMB OCTAGON BARN AGRICULTURAL MUSEUM

WHAT: The largest octagon barn in North America

WHERE: 6948 Richie Rd., Gagetown

COST: Donation

PRO TIP: Plan to spend approximately an hour and a half to see all the additional buildings and the Purdy home.

Gagetown residents organized to save the barn. They discovered the barn was on the Michigan State Registry of Historic Sites as the "Round Barn," so it couldn't be taken down. During that time, a Tuscola County organization, Tuscola 2001, took an active interest in saving the barn. Fundraising efforts drew attention to the project, and the Friends of the Thumb Octagon Barn, working with the DNR, agreed to begin restoration of the buildings. Today, they are a 501(c)3 tax-exempt nonprofit corporation and continue adding more historic buildings to the property. The property is becoming a complete agricultural museum.

The property includes about a dozen additional historic structures, including a covered bridge, a one-room schoolhouse, a blacksmith shop, a cider mill, a grain elevator, the powerhouse, and the Purdy home furnished as it was when they lived there.

A view of the Octagon Barn from the balcony of the Purdy home. Photo courtesy of Alexis Dingman.

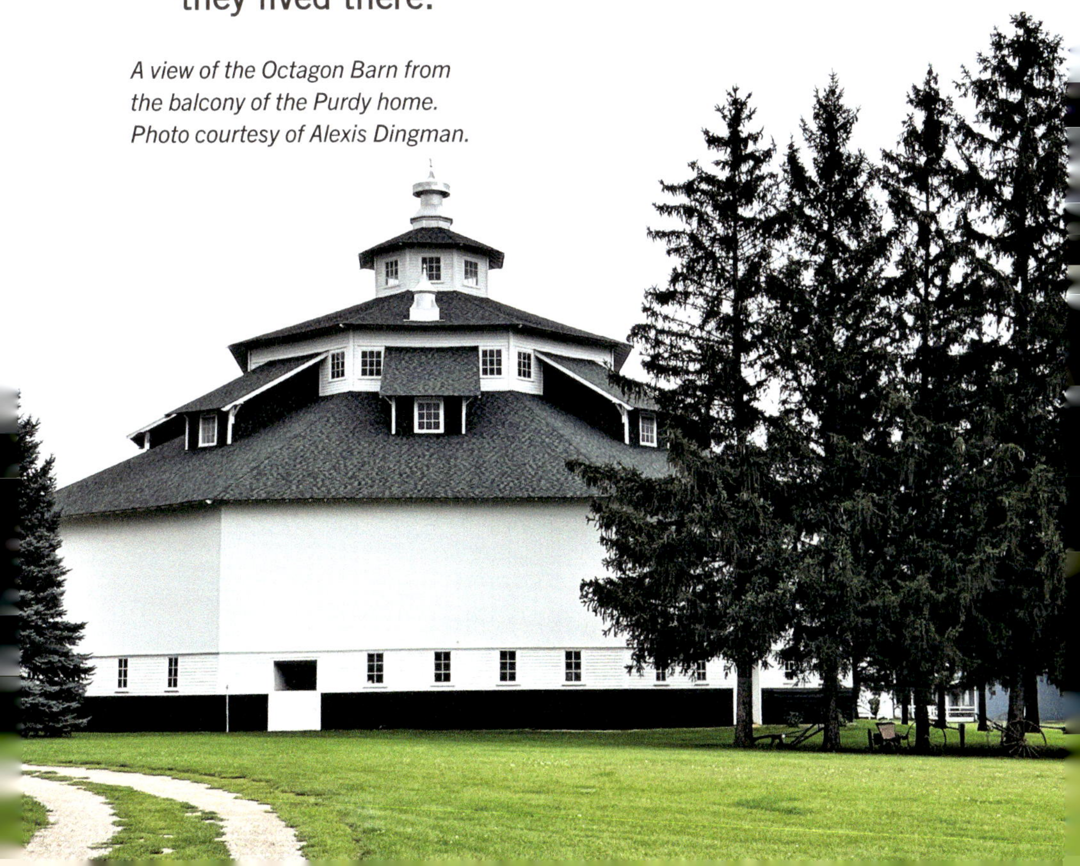

YULE BE AMAZED

What is the world's largest Christmas store's secret to building a staff known for excellent customer service?

Bronner's CHRISTmas Wonderland, the world's largest year-round Christmas store, is as big as 1.7 football fields or 2.2 acres. And that's just the store itself! The landscaped grounds cover over 27 acres. Bronner's gets you into the Christmas spirit year-round by lighting up Bronner's half-mile Christmas Lane every evening from dusk until midnight with about 100,000 lights. Their average electric bill is $1,250 per day!

So how does such a large store build a staff known for excellent customer service? While celebrating the season's joy 361 days a year, Bronner's strives to have all their visitors, whether in-store, online, or over the phone, experience the magic of CHRISTmas while visiting. Over two million guests visit Bronner's annually, including 2,000 tour groups. For each of those visitors, their vision focuses on a desire to provide a positive customer experience. At Bronner's, they like to take things a step further to exceed—rather than meet—expectations. Their customer service is about maintaining that positive attitude at all times. They listen patiently and communicate with their customers. They believe the customers keep the wonder in their wonderland. Check their website under

---

Bonner's Silent Night Memorial Chapel is a replica of the original in Oberndorf, Salzburg, Austria. The chapel in Austria was where they sang "Silent Night" on Christmas Eve in 1818 for the first time. Open during store hours for visitation and meditation. The chapel is not available for ceremonies.

Top: *Nativity scene outside of Bronner's CHRISTmas Wonderland in Frankenmuth.*
Inset: *Christmas Ornaments at the world's largest Christmas store.*

group tours for coupons. Plan to spend about two and a half hours shopping and experiencing Bronner's customer service.

BRONNER'S CHRISTMAS WONDERLAND

WHAT: The largest Christmas store in the world

WHERE: 25 Christmas Ln., Frankenmuth

COST: Free to shop. Prices vary based on selection.

PRO TIP: Visit Bronner's website. At the bottom of the page under Just for Fun, click on the Coloring Pages link.

Castle Farms
Photo courtesy of Castle Farms

SOURCES

God Save the King: beaverislandhistory.org/print-shop; The Beaver Island Historical Society. *Beaver Island: A Brief History.* Escanaba: The Beaver Island Historical Society, 2007.; Historical Markers on Beaver Island; Harvey, Miles. *The King of Confidence.* New York: Little, Brown and Company, 2021.

Hail to the Chief: fordlibrarymuseum.gov/index.aspx

The Sisterhood of Dolls: crossinthewoods.com/doll-museum; tributearchive.com/obituaries/2329198/Sally-Gloria-Rogalski; Conversation with Jim Nowak, Shrine Director, on May 9, 2023

The Secret Garden: brysestate.com; Conversation with Kathryn Brys at the vineyard on May 1, 2023

The Shoreline's Tiny Treasure Is in Peril: nps.gov/slbe/learn/nature/pipingplover.htm; greatlakespipingplover.org; fws.gov/species/piping-plover-charadrius-melodus; Tour with Sleeping Bear Tour Co. and conversation with tour guide Julie Den Uyl on May 21, 2023

A Place of Healing: thevillagetc.com; Tours of the Village at Grand Traverse Commons and conversation with teour guide Kate Angove on May 3, 2023, and the Visual History Presentation with tour guide Joe Kilpatrick on May 23, 2023

From Spirituality to Baseball: facebook.com/profile.php?id=100050234477825&sk=about; hodfilm.com; Conversation with Chris Siriano and tour of the House of David Museum on May 20, 2023

From Agriculture to Architecture: castlefarms.com; savingplaces.org/distinctive-destinations/castle-farms

Picture This: michigan.gov/mhc/museums/sanilac

A Symphony of Nature: landtrust.org/wp-content/uploads/2021/01/Agnes-S-Andreae-Nature-Preserve-Nature-Megaphone.pdf

Driven by Beauty: gilmorecarmuseum.org

From Bars to Brushes: experiencejackson.com/meet/group-tour-options/group-prison-tours; historicprisontours.com; Conversation with Jim Guerriero and tour of the Jackson Historic Prison on May 26, 2023

When Cadillac Was Kissed: cadillacmichigan.com/a-new-chapter-in-cadillacs-kisstory; youtube.com/watch?v=j2U8kG7LRuo; kisscadillac.com; s26514.pcdn.co/wp-content/uploads/2020/09/2020KISS-WebPrint-v2.pdf

Flying High at the Zoo: airzoo.org

Oh, Hell Yes!: gotohellmi.com; The author was mayor of Hell for a day on June 13, 2023.

A Light with Wanderlust: michigan.gov/mhc/museums/tawas/visitor-information; www.tawaslighthousefriends.com; hmdb.org/m.asp?m=123999

A Leg Up: legsinn.com; youtube.com/watch?v=ulTTptfxMoU&t=42s

It's Not Freezing: cadillacmichigan.com/2-lakes-a-canal-a-railroad-a-bit-of-history; cadillacmichigan.com/the-mystery-of-the-canal

Gnome Sweet Gnome: visitcharlevoix.com/earl-young; Miles, David L. Boulders: *The Life and Creations of Earl A. Young in Charlevoix, Michigan*. Charlevoix: Charlevoix Historical Society Press, 2020.

Back from the Brink: michiganaudubon.org/kirtlands-warbler-tours; michigan.gov/dnr/education/michigan-species/plants-trees/jackpine; fs.usda.gov/recarea/hmnf/recarea/?recid=19002; audubon.org/field-guide/bird/kirtlands-warbler

Beyond the Badge: copsdoughnuts.com; Stanton, Anne. *Cops and Doughnuts*. Traverse City: Mission Point Press, 2022.; Cops & Doughnuts Bakery: Nine Cops to the Rescue. Pamphlet

Lost in the Depths: thunderbay.noaa.gov; thunderbayfriends.org; mff.forest.mtu.edu/PDF/1-TreeBasics/3-History.pdf; Tour with Shipwreck Tours on June 25, 2023

Farm to Table: lcculinary.org

Digging Deep: mackinacparks.com/more-info/history/archaeology/colonial-michilimackinac-archaeology

The Steel Chronicles: mightymac.org/bridgemuseum.htm

Into the Wild: gaylordmichigan.net/member/gaylords-city-elk-park; gaylordmichigan.net/member/pigeon-river-country-state-forest; michigan.gov/-/media/Project/Websites/dnr/Documents/Brochures/DNR_Elk_Brochure.pdf

Nature's Sculpture: portaustinkayak.com/turnip-rock; portaustinarea.com/turnip-rock

The Flavor of History: mammothdistilling.com/rosen; Conversation with Stuart Hickman at the Mammoth Distilling tasting room in Traverse City on May 1, 2023

Prehistoric Paradise: dinosaurgardensllc.com

A Ferry Tale: ssbadger.com

Big Spring, Bigger Marvel: michigandnr.com/parksandtrails/Details.aspx?id=425&type=SPRK

Rooted in Beauty: m119tunneloftrees.org/default.asp; m119tunneloftrees.org/downloads/m119_guidebook.pdf; m119tunneloftrees.org/preserve.asp; is0.gaslightmedia.com/petoskeyareacvb/_ORIGINAL_/fs16-1316027561-57857.pdf

Petrified Perfection: petoskeyarea.com/play/petoskey-stone-hunting; michigan.org/article/trip-idea/where-find-petoskey-stones-michigan

My Hands Are Clean: moisttowelettemuseum.com

Lost with the Lumber: hmdb.org/m.asp?m=45269; saugatuckduneride.com/home.html; hmdb.org/m.asp?m=45269

From Crisis to Conservation: michigan.gov/mhc/museums/hln-ccc; michigan.gov/mhc/museums/hln-ccc/ccc-in-michigan

Quills and Thrills: www2.dnr.state.mi.us/parksandtrails/Details.aspx?id=426&type=SPRK; michigan.org/property/porcupine-mountains-wilderness-state-park

History Meets Hospitality: cartiermansion.com; historicwhitepinevillage.org; web.archive.org/web/20141104074955/http://mynorth.com/2009/02/the-life-of-ludingtons-cartier-mansion/3

Rock-Solid Beauty: nps.gov/piro/planyourvisit/index.htm; picturedrocks.com

The Never-Ending Job: mackinacbridge.org; https://www.freep.com/story/news/local/michigan/2017/11/01/mackinac-bridge-facts/793165001/; northernexpress.com/news/feature/refurbishing-a-jewel-how-to-paint-the-mackinac-bridge

Ain't I a Woman?: nps.gov/people/sojourner-truth.htm; battlecreekvisitors.org/wp-content/uploads/2022/06/2022_VisitorGuide_FinalFull_Web.pdf; battlecreekvisitors.org/meet-sojourner-truth-a-michigan-heroine

An Elevated Experience: boynemountain.com/skybridge-michigan

Beyond Nuts and Bolts: wkfr.com/worlds-largest-lug-nut; atlasobscura.com/places/world-s-largest-lug-nut; witl.com/the-story-of-the-giant-lugnut-watching-over-downtown-lansing; mentalfloss.com/article/55767/how-lansing-lugnuts-got-their-name; oursportscentral.com/services/releases/america-votes-lugnuts-are-1-minor-league-nickname/n-3059103

A Passport to Change: hmdb.org/m.asp?m=134565; history.com/news/8-little-known-facts-about-the-peace-corps

Battling Cherry Pie Pans: atlasobscura.com/places/former-worlds-largest-cherry-pie-pan; atlasobscura.com/places/worlds-largest-cherry-pie-tin

Chillax with a Book: americanchillers.com

Wheel Turned Tire: clickondetroit.com/all-about-michigan/2018/07/04/history-behind-michigans-uniroyal-giant-tire-on-i-94; hagerty.com/media/automotive-history/detroits-giant-uniroyal-tire-is-a-kind-of-big-wheel-that-tells-a-very-big-story

Reptilian Retreat: alligatorsanctuary.wixsite.com/alligatorsanctuary

Trash to Treasure: americanmuseumofmagic.com

Gizzards Galore: gizzardcity.com

Field of Honor: wellplannedadventures.com/blog/visiting-the-poppy-field-at-pleasant-hill-farm; wzzm13.com/article/news/local/michigan-life/fennville-farming-couple-field-of-poppies-flowers/69-aa0bf5c9-0dfa-450a-bcfa-18d1a55ab742; hollandsentinel.com/story/news/2020/06/18/fennville-family-commemorates-late-son-with-field-of-poppies/114281090

What You Know, You Know: visitmanisteecounty.com/web-2-0-directory/ramsdell-regional-center-for-the-arts; visitmanisteecounty.com/web-2-0-directory/the-ramsdell-theatre

Flouting the Dry Spell: thrillist.com/venue/drink/detroit/bar/two-way-inn; audacy.com/wwjnewsradio/news/local/beer-wine-and-spirits-the-oldest-bar-in-detroit-may-also-be-the-most-haunted; metrotimes.com/news/a-spirit-of-detroit-2192081

Flour Power: youtube.com/watch?v=qj3bz86sbH8; cityofholland.com/535/De-Zwaan-Windmill

From Author's Haven to Historic Landmark: owossohistory.org

Retro Rarities: yankeeairmuseum.org

Respect and Remember: miheroes.org

Luge Your Mind: msports.org/muskegon-winter-luge-track

Timeless Vigilance: visitmanisteecounty.com/web-2-0-directory/manistee-fire-hall; manisteemi.gov/DocumentCenter/View/2302/Fire-Dept-History; sites.rootsweb.com/~mimanist/ManHist14.html

Remember the Raisin!: nps.gov/rira/index.htm

From Cocoa to Curds: frankenmuthcheesehaus.com

Lyrical Landmark: infomi.com/city/reedcity/museum.html; staugustine.com/story/lifestyle/faith/2017/10/21/story-behind-song-old-rugged-cross/16290488007; lifeway.com/en/articles/the-history-behind-the-old-rugged-cross-hymn-george-bennard-revival

Mechanical Marvels: marvin3m.com; marvin3m.com/?page_id=35

The Otherside Unveiled: facebook.com/profile.php?id=100092632395681

No Cars Allowed: mlive.com/entertainment/erry-2018/03/797a7e7b1b/a_guide_to_michigans_m185_the.html; www.triplepundit.com/story/2013/mackinac-island-where-cars-are-banned-and-bikes-rule-road/48911; michigan.gov/mdot/0%2C1607%2C7-151-9620_11154-129683--%2C00.html

Ghostly Footprints: mittenbrewing.com/ghost-files

All Aboard: durandstation.org; *Depot Dreams: A Compilation of Stories, Life, and History of Durand Union Station*. Edited and composed by Brian J. Boggs and Dr. M. Jean Sloan, 2005

From Skeletons to Spirits: anatomyofdeathmuseum.com

Unlocking the Mystery: originalsoolocktours.com; saultstemarie.com/attractions/soo-locks

Seeing Things: facebook.com/TheMioPizzaShop; wbxxfm.com/michigans-giant-pink-elephants; roadsideamerica.com/tip/54657

Listen to the Trees: ipf.msu.edu/hidden-lake-gardens; jackwiklebonsailegacy.com/?page_id=904

Small Wonders: midwestminiaturesmuseum.com

Galactic Getaways: michigan.org/darksky; keweenawmountainlodge.com/activities/stargazing; keweenawdarksky.com

Pretty as a Picture: lansingstatejournal.com/story/life/2018/08/21/stunning-lobby-bwl-dye-water-plant-blow-you-away/1017848002

Vintage Views and Vino: chateauchantal.com

Urban Oasis: www2.dnr.state.mi.us/parksandtrails/Details.aspx?id=736&type=SPRK

Upcycling at Its Best: visitmanisteecounty.com/web-2-0-directory/kaleva-bottle-house-museum; kalevamichigan.com

The Roaring River: www2.dnr.state.mi.us/parksandtrails/Details.aspx?id=428&type=SPRK

Yes, Captain!: southhavenlight.org

Illusions and Enchantment: tripadvisor.com/Attraction_Review-g42095-d21311098-Reviews-Lakeside_Cemetery-Colon_St_Joseph_County_Michigan.html; A conversation with Joe Ganger at the Community Historical Museum

A Bright Idea: phmuseum.org/thomas-edison-depot-museum

A Secret Passage: castlemuseum.org

From Eight to Great: thumboctagonbarn.org

Yule Be Amazed: bronners.com

Male Kirtland's warbler
Photo courtesy of Michigan Audubon

INDEX